PONTIAC
CLASSICS

PONTIAC
CLASSICS

BY THE AUTO EDITORS OF CONSUMER GUIDE®

Publications International, Ltd.

Louis Weber, CEO
Publications International, Ltd.
7373 North Cicero Avenue
Lincolnwood, Illinois 60712

Permission is never granted for commercial purposes.

ISBN-13: 978-1-60553-376-6
ISBN-10: 1-60553-376-9

Manufactured in China.

8 7 6 5 4 3 2 1

Library of Congress Control Number: 2009939531

Credits

Photography:
The editors would like to thank the following people for supplying the photography that made this book possible. They are listed below, along with the page number(s) of their photos.

Roger Barnes: 113; **Scott Brandt:** 47; **Robert H. Brown:** 107; **Gary Cameron:** 101; **Jeff Cohn:** 37; **Thomas Glatch:** 85, 91, 105; **Sam Griffith:** 15, 17, 53, 89; **Don Heiny:** 119; **Brandon Hemphill:** 67; **Bud Juneau:** 33, 39, 103; **Milton Kieft:** 27, 69; **Nick Komic:** 49, 57; **Dan Lyons:** 35, 97, 125; **Vince Manocchi:** 13, 43, 51, 61, 71, 83, 111, 121; **Doug Mitchel:** 19, 21, 29, 59, 65, 75, 95, 99, 109, 117; **Ron Moorhead:** 41; **Jeff Rose:** 93; **Gary Smith:** 73; **Richard Spiegelman:** 123; **Alex Steinberg:** 9; **David Temple:** 11, 55; **W.C. Waymack:** 23, 45, 63, 79, 87; **Nicky Wright:** 25, 31; **Paul Zazarine:** 81

Back Cover: Jeff Cohn; Sam Griffith; Richard Spiegelman; David Temple; Nicky Wright

Owners:
Special thanks to the owners of the cars featured in this book for their cooperation. Their names and the page number(s) for their vehicles follow.

Mike Abbott: 95; **Walter & Darlene Abela:** 57; **Bill & Kathy Berks:** 51; **Jim Bombard:** 35; **Lionel Boulin:** 101; **Mike Callahan:** 23; **Chevs n' Vettes, Inc.:** Back cover, 25; Dick Choler: 31; **Robert & Karen Christanell:** 47; **Jerry Coffee:** Back cover, 55; **Dr. Randy & Freda Cooper:** 61, 71; **Marc Cruji:** Back cover, 123; **Custom Automotive Services:** 49; **Patrick & Barbara Dugan:** 97; **Tim Dunlop:** 93; **Roland C. Eggebrecht:** 91; **Neil Ehresman:** 103; **Fred Engers:** 89; **Mike Ford:** 119; **General Motors:** 127; **Mario Gutierrez:** 41; **Tom Hall:** Back cover, 15, 17; **William Hamann:** 105; **Glenn Hammack:** Back cover, 37; **John Hammel:** 45; **Garth Higgins:** 43; **Paul and Roy Jaszczak:** 9; **E.J. & Rachelle Jaymeson:** 121; **Michael & Patricia Kelso:** 53; **Don & Cheryl Knowland:** 63; **Larry Lange:** 19; **Jim Lee:** 83; **Fred Lewis:** 21; **Dan & Joyce Lyons:** 125; **Philip Manoanici:** 111; **James & Sandy Marcellus:** 73; **Richard & Madeline Martindale:** 69; **Paul & Peg Mather:** 27; **Bob Mayer:** 117; **Jim McGrew:** 11; **Michael Merritt:** 75; **Harold Miller:** 79; **John & Pat Mueller:** 87; **Jerrold V. Murphy:** 67; **Richard Parente:** 81; **Leonard Redford:** 13; **Si Rogers:** 85; **Larry Rowen:** 115; **Glyn & Jan Rowley:** 39; **John Sanders:** 29; **Steve Schappaugh:** 113; **John Skwirblies:** 109; **Gary Smith:** 65; **Ralph Stegall:** 59; **Jim & Stacey Swarbrick:** 99; **June Trumbley:** 33; **Donald P. Vrabec:** 107; **Bob Williford:** 77

CONTENTS

FOREWORD

Pontiac was born out of General Motors executive Alfred P. Sloan's reorganization of the company's product line in the early Twenties. The pragmatic Sloan determined GM needed a car line priced above Chevrolet but below Oldsmobile, and the result was the 1926 Pontiac. Those first models were essentially little more than a contemporary Chevy with a six-cylinder engine instead of a four under the hood.

The new car was sold by the struggling Oakland Division of GM. Pontiac quickly prospered in the market and overshadowed Oakland; the latter was history after 1931. But by the Fifties, Oldsmobile was outselling Pontiac by a substantial margin.

When Semon "Bunkie" Knudsen took over as the Division's general manager in July 1956, Pontiac's

dowdy image soon gave way to a confident swagger and seemingly ever-increasing sales. Performance and style became Pontiac hallmarks. With products like the Bonneville, Grand Prix, GTO, and Trans Am, beautiful advertising art, and memorable terms like "Wide Track" and "Ram Air," Pontiac owned a mystique that few other marques could hope to match. Over time, Pontiac had trouble adapting to the ever-changing automobile market and lost its edge, but flashes of greatness were visible right to the end.

Pontiac Classics celebrates some of the marque's finest hours, pairing historic advertisements with stunning photographs. It's a colorful tribute to the best of the breed.

A NEW SIX— A NEW NAME A NEW VALUE

AFTER a long period of preparation, General Motors now presents the lowest priced high quality Six. This newest member of a famous family is an entirely new car, embodying the full scope of the corporation's resources in engineering, purchasing and production. It will be manufactured and distributed by the Oakland division as companion car to the new Oakland Six. . . . Into this field, where low price has hitherto been the chief inducement to ownership, the Pontiac Six introduces elements of size, beauty, comfort, stamina, roadability and completeness of equipment that are literally and truthfully without precedent. . . . Notwithstanding these extraordinary qualities, the Pontiac Six will sell for a price so unexpectedly low as to compel a radical rearrangement of every existing idea of motor car value.

GENERAL SPECIFICATIONS

ENGINE—Own design and make 6-cylinder, L-head type, water-cooled by pump circulation. Bore, 3¼ inches. Stroke, 3¾ inches, displacement, 186.50 cubic inches. Three-point suspension; two detachable cylinder heads.

CYLINDERS—Cast in block of special cylinder iron, integral with crankcase. Flywheel enclosed. All cylinders have glass-like finish obtained by honing process. Cylinders and valves completely surrounded by circulating water.

CRANKSHAFT—Three-bearing type, statically and dynamically balanced. Bearing sizes: front, 1 15/16 inches diameter by 1⅝ inches; center, 2-inch diameter by 2 inches; rear, 2 1/16 inches by 2 inches. Patented bronze-backed, babbitt-lined, interchangeable main bearings.

CAMSHAFT—Drop-forged steel, integral cams, case-hardened and ground. Bearing sizes: front, 1 15/16-inch diameter by 1½ inches; center, 1 13/16-inch diameter by 1⅛ inches; rear, 1⅝-inch diameter by 1 1/16 inches. Lubrication by special oil pockets and splash system. Silent drive with 1¼-inch chain.

PISTONS—Light semi-steel 4 inches long with three 3/16-inch cast iron rings. Piston pin, 1 1/16-inch diameter, locked in piston.

CONNECTING RODS—Drop-forged, heat-treated, I-beam section, 7 5/16 inches long. Lower bearing, 2-inch diameter by 1 3/16 inches; upper bushings, 1 1/16-inch diameter by 1 5/16 inches, bronze; lower bearing high grade babbitt, accurately broached to size.

VALVES—High temperature resisting silicon-chromium steel. Accessible for grinding by removing head. Diameter, 1 7/16 inches. Tappets have chilled cast iron head with long-wearing steel sleeve. Self oiling, mushroom type valve lifters.

LUBRICATION SYSTEM—Of special design known as regulated constant flow type; pressure being taken care of by adjustable pressure release valve. Pressure feed from gear driven pump to all main bearings and connecting rods. Submerged gear type oil pump gear driven at center bearing. Valve compartment open to splash. Valve chamber provided with oil-tight coverings. Pressure gauge on instrument board. Oil filter located on left side of engine with oil level gauge rod nearby. Oil capacity, 6½ quarts. Pressure oil lubrication and fittings for chassis.

GASOLINE—Vacuum tank system. 12-gallon tank in rear provided with gauge unit.

INTAKE MANIFOLD—Special design utilizing exhaust heat from 5 cylinders in maintaining correct temperature for carburetor inlet. Perfect volatilization and mechanical distribution.

CARBURETOR—Carter, 1-inch.

ELECTRICAL SYSTEM—Remy starting, lighting and ignition. Motor with Bendix drive. Generator, third brush current regulation. Automatic distributor. 6-volt, 80-ampere power storage battery. 21 candle power, diffusing lens, head lamps. Side lamps for parking. Approved rear light. Combination light and ignition switch with lock for locking ignition.

COOLING SYSTEM—Water; impeller pump; cellular type, high turbulence radiator, with polished nickel shell. Two-blade fan on pump shaft, 15 inches in diameter. Capacity, 10½ quarts.

CLUTCH—Dry single disc type, ventilated and self adjusting. One driven and two driving discs. Driven disc faced with long wearing friction lining. Outside diameter, 9 inches. Eight pressure springs; pedal adjustable to compensate wear.

TRANSMISSION—Unit-power plant type, selective sliding; 3 speeds forward and reverse. Gears of heat-treated chrome-vanadium steel accurately cut and shaped. New Departure ball bearings for pinion shaft and main driving shaft. Bronze bushings for counter gears.

FRAME—Pressed steel channel section, 4½ inches deep; 1¾ inches wide. Straight side members. Tapers from front to rear. Four cross members including rear engine support. Over-all length, 153 3/32 inches.

STEERING GEAR—Semi-reversible worm and wheel type, 16-inch wheel. 8 to 1 ratio to provide easy steering. Horn button at top of steering wheel.

INSTRUMENT PANEL—Indirect illumination. Instrument group includes 75-mile speedometer, ammeter, oil pressure gauge, throttle and choke control windshield cleaner regulator and ignition and lighting switch with lock.

FRONT AXLE—Own make, drop-forged I-beam section. Springs over axle. Steering knuckles of special alloy steel. New Departure bearings for wheel spindles.

REAR AXLE—Own make, semi-floating type, banjo housing with torque tube connected to front end of pinion housing. Chrome nickel steel pinion and ring gear. New Departure ball bearings used throughout.

WHEELS—Heavy artillery type equipped with 20 x 4 inches rims.

TIRES—Low pressure balloon cords, 29 x 4.75 inches, non-skid tread.

BRAKES—Service brakes on rear wheels. Drum diameter, 11 inches; width of brake, 2 inches. Adjusted and equalized. Parking brake on rear wheels, internal expanding; operated by hand lever.

SPRINGS—Semi-elliptic, front and rear. Length of front spring, 36 inches; width, 1¾ inches. Length of rear spring, 54 inches; width, 1¾ inches. Front spring special quality carbon steel. Rear spring, chrome-vanadium steel. Hard rolled bronze bushings in spring eyes.

TURNING RADIUS—19 feet 4 inches.

WHEELBASE—110 inches.

ROAD CLEARANCE—8½ inches.

BODY—Built by Fisher.

UPHOLSTERY—Coupe and Coach: Cushions in long wearing gray corduroy; balance interior in art weave upholstering cloth to match.

BODY EQUIPMENT—Coupe: Sun visor, landau bows on rear quarter, double beading. Plate glass windows, high speed window regulators. Fisher VV one-piece windshield, rear vision mirror, automatic windshield cleaner, roller shade over rear window, safety lock on right door with inside snap lock on left door. Coach: Sun visor, double beading, plate glass windows, high speed window regulators on doors and quarter windows, Fisher VV one-piece windshield, rear vision mirror, foot rest, floor carpets, dome light, automatic windshield cleaner, roller shade over rear window, safety lock on front door with inside snap lock on left door.

WEIGHTS—Car ready for road: Coupe, 2320 pounds: Coach, 2400 pounds.

P O N T I A C

"CHIEF OF THE SIXES"

1926
SERIES 6-27

For 1926, General Motors introduced a new brand that adopted the name of the Michigan city where it was built: Pontiac. The low-cost six-cylinder automobile was intended to cover a price gap between Chevrolet and Oldsmobile in the corporation's product hierarchy. Engineering for the new car was handled by Chevrolet, but Pontiacs were built and sold by the Oakland division of GM. The Pontiac shared many parts with the contemporary Chevrolet and used a 36-horsepower 186.5-cubic-inch six in Chevy's 110-inch-wheelbase chassis. In its first year, only two Pontiac models were offered: a two-passenger coupe and a five-passenger coach. Both listed for $825. Nearly 77,000 were sold in 1926; from 1927 to 1933, Pontiac was fifth in industry sales. Oakland's last year was 1931.

The Cabriolet, list price at Pontiac, Michigan, $860*

LOOK AT THE NEW PONTIAC EIGHT
Only $715 *

Now you're looking at the car you're always wanted . . . the new PONTIAC EIGHT . . . eight cylinders at their *smoothest* and *best.* . . . And a beauty . . . acclaimed at the New York Show as "*one of the two most beautiful cars in America.*". . . Big, powerful, and ruggedly *dependable,* this new Pontiac has an 84-horsepower engine, capable of 85 thrilling miles an hour. Many owners report 16 to 18 miles

to the gallon of gas. Remarkable economy! . . . Smarter, roomier Fisher Body . . . Perfection Bendix brakes, and the new Enclosed Knee-Action Wheel springing that gives you the greatest *riding ease* and *comfort* you have ever enjoyed. . . . Go *see* this new Pontiac . . . *examine* it . . . *ride* in it. Today!

* List prices at Pontiac, Michigan, $715 and up. With bumpers, spare tire, metal tire cover, tire lock and spring covers, the list price is $32.00 additional. . . . Pontiac is a General Motors Value.

PONTIAC
Get a Pontiac Eight for your money

1934
EIGHT

The 1934 Pontiacs sported mildly restyled bodies on a 2.5-inch-longer wheelbase. All used the 223.4-cubic-inch straight eight that was introduced for 1933, but carburetion and cylinder-head improvements boosted horse-power from 77 to 84. Pontiac's version of GM's "Knee Action" independent front suspension featured a different design than that used by Buick, Cadillac, and Oldsmobile, and it proved to be less reliable. A new design replaced it by 1937. The sport coupe (shown here) listed for $725 and came standard with a rumble seat and a single rear-mounted spare tire. The dual side-mount spares were optional. Pontiac's model-year production fell 21 percent to 78,859 units. Still, this tally was good enough for a fifth-place ranking in industry output.

A **Low-priced Six**
whose quality makes the price
Phenomenal

ONLY FROM A PLANT SO
MODERN COULD COME
A LOW-PRICED CAR
SO FINE

THE MOST BEAUTIFUL THING ON WHEELS

If it is your habit to compare before buying, please change your usual method when you come to the new Pontiac Six. Compare it, by all means, but *not* with cars in its *own* price range. Measure it, instead, against *the costliest cars of the day*. Despite its low price you will find that its quality ranks with the finest! There are no better bodies than "Turret-Top" Bodies by Fisher, whose solid-steel roof, welded to steel sides, makes them the safest in the world. Money

cannot buy better brakes than Pontiac's big hydraulics—triple-sealed against dirt and moisture. The six, as Pontiac builds it, successfully combines smoother, livelier performance with even greater economy. And, of course, the car America christened *the most beautiful thing on wheels* will more than hold its own in appearance. So compare—and insist on quality. If you want to stay in the low-price range, you are bound to decide—you can't do better than a *Pontiac Six*.

HIGHLIGHTS OF PONTIAC QUALITY FOR 1935
• • •
Solid Steel "Turret-Top" Bodies by Fisher • Triple-Sealed Hydraulic Brakes • Speedlined Styling • Completely Sealed Chassis • Silver-Alloy Bearing Engines • 10-Second Starting at Zero • Even Greater Economy • No Draft Ventilation • *Knee-Action • Luggage and Spare Tire Compartment.

PONTIAC MOTOR COMPANY, PONTIAC, MICHIGAN. *Division of General Motors*

 NEW PONTIAC SIXES *and* EIGHTS **$615**

*AND UP. List price of Standard six-cylinder Coupe at Pontiac, Michigan. Standard group of accessories extra. *On the Eight and De Luxe Six Models.*

1935
EIGHT

The new-for-1935 Pontiac was a more stream-lined, Art Deco machine that ushered in a design cue destined to be a trademark for the division for more than 20 years: designer Franklin Hershey's famed "Silver Streak." The Sliver Streak treatment began as a bright band of multiple ribs running from the base of the windshield and across the hood, which then dropped down to form the center section of a somewhat streamlined waterfall grille. The body itself was based on the General Motors "A" body and used Fisher Body's new all-steel "turret top" for coupes and sedans. The full use of "suicide" rear-hinged doors on every model was a somewhat retrograde feature. Returning eight-cylinder models like this Touring sedan were newly joined by two lines of sixes.

If you want the extra smoothness, extra performance and extra luxury of a big, fine-quality, 8-cylinder car ... if you want that eight to embody all the good things General Motors stands for ... and if you want all this at the lowest possible price, you'll end up by driving a Pontiac! Because this gorgeous Silver Streaked beauty with its 198″ over-all length, and its superbly silent and efficient engine, is the one car in all the world measuring up to those exacting requirements!

BIGGER CAR
BETTER VALUE
GREATER ECONOMY

Pontiac
GENERAL MOTORS' LOWEST PRICED 8

1937
DeLUXE EIGHT

Pontiacs wore a new "face" for 1937, with horizontal grille sections bisected by the "Silver Streak" waterfall chrome trim. Phaetons were fading from the automotive scene in the late 1930s, so it seems odd that Pontiac added a convertible sedan to its lineup. It was available in both DeLuxe Six and DeLuxe Eight form. Pontiac interiors featured clean, streamlined dashboards with an attractive rectangular gauge cluster and a unique spherical ashtray on the glovebox door. Both Pontiac engines gained horsepower and displacement for 1937. The six now put out 85 horses from 222.7 cubic inches, while the eight displaced 248.9 cubic inches and made an even 100 ponies. Pontiac had its best sales year yet as model-year output climbed 34 percent to 236,189.

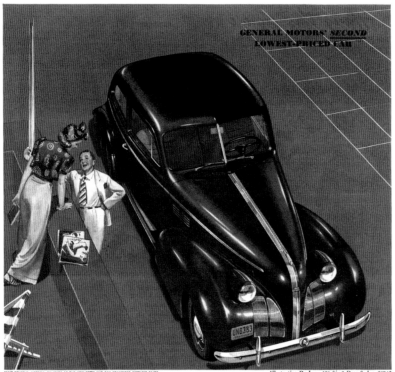

VISIT GENERAL MOTORS' EXHIBITS AT THE NEW YORK AND SAN FRANCISCO WORLD'S FAIRS

Illustrating De Luxe 120 Six 2-Door Sedan, $871*

Pontiac Has a Purpose All Its Own

If you think of Pontiac as merely another motor car, you are making a serious mistake. For Pontiac has a special mission in life and is built to meet a very specific need. It is built for those hundreds of thousands of motorists who want a low-priced, economical car—but who want more comfort, beauty, safety, performance and wheel-base than the lowest-price field affords.

Pontiac has been called the perfect answer to this requirement. Certainly, it has no serious competitor in the field it has made so peculiarly its own. Look at Pontiac before you choose a motor car. You'll find that you want everything it offers—and you'll also find that it offers everything you want!

PONTIAC $758

GENERAL MOTORS TERMS TO SUIT YOUR PURSE

AND UP, *delivered at Pontiac, Mich., subject to change without notice. Transportation, state and local taxes (if any), optional equipment, accessories—extra.*

1939
DeLUXE EIGHT

New-for-1939 Pontiac DeLuxe Six and DeLuxe Eight bodies wore wider "pontoon" fenders and streamlined noses with chromed "catwalk" grilles. A new low-cost "Quality Six" line debuted, wearing a Chevrolet bodyshell fitted with Pontiac front sheetmetal. Though not instantly noticeable, another of the 1939 Pontiac's design highlights was its new "alligator-jaw" hood. Today, the vast majority of cars have hoods that are hinged at the firewall and lift up from the front, but previous Pontiacs and most other cars of the era featured hoods that opened from the sides. The $1046 DeLuxe Eight convertible shown here was the only 1939 Pontiac to break the $1000 price barrier. Model-year production rose 48.5 percent to 144,340, which was good for sixth overall in industry output.

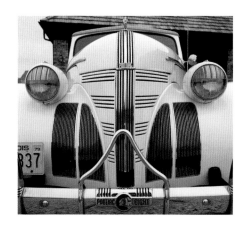

Special Six 4-Door Touring Sedan, $884*
There's superlative comfort in its wide seats and "Triple-Cushioned" ride

Special Six 2-Door Touring Sedan, $830*
A big, luxurious Pontiac sedan priced right down with the lowest

Special Six Sport Coupe, $827*
Has a full-width, full-cushioned rear seat for occasional guests
(This model also available on De Luxe Six and De Luxe Eight chassis)

Special Six Business Coupe, $783*
Built for extra-rugged service and lowest operating cost

It's Spring - and Summer's Just Around the Corner
- Pick Out Your *Pontiac!*

IT'S AN OLD, and exciting, American custom to meet Spring more than halfway in a fresh, sparkling, new motor car.

To help you make your 1940 Spring selection, Pontiac portrays on these pages eleven of its seventeen 1940 models.

It will make you feel better all over to take to the road in one of these big, wide-seated, long-wheelbase beauties—especially after driving a smaller car. Feel the smoothness of that power-packed Pontiac engine. Feel the comfort of that Pontiac "Triple-Cushioned" ride. And enjoy the luxury that surrounds you in Pontiac's "big car" interior.

And when you get a check on the *economy* of operating a Pontiac, you'll really begin to realize what a marvelous car you've bought. For records prove that Pontiac issues a very defiant economy challenge to even the smallest cars.

The biggest thrill, of course, is the Pontiac price. It's in easy reach of everyone, *right down with the lowest!*

Delivered at Pontiac, Mich. Transportation based on rail rates, state and local taxes (if any), optional equipment and accessories—extra. Prices subject to change without notice. General Motors terms to suit your purse.

De Luxe Eight 2-Door Touring Sedan, $919*
(And there's an equally charming De Luxe Six 2-Door Sedan)

De Luxe Six 4-Door Touring Sedan, $940*
Two-tone finish as illustrated available on any Pontiac model at no extra cost
(Same model on De Luxe Eight chassis priced slightly higher)

De Luxe Six Business Coupe, $835*
(Pontiac also builds the Business Coupe on the De Luxe Eight chassis)

De Luxe Six Cabriolet, $1011*
Colored upholstery in leather or leather and whipcord—
to harmonize with body and top colors
(This model also available on De Luxe Eight chassis)

Station Wagon, $1015*
Carries eight in comfort—Rides like a Sedan

"Torpedo" Eight 4-Door Touring Sedan, $1092*
Acknowledged Leader of the 1940 Style Parade!
(Two-tone finish as illustrated optional on any Pontiac model at slight extra cost)

"Torpedo" Eight Sport Coupe, $1026*
A personal car designed to make your motoring more delightful

1940
SPECIAL SIX

For 1940, another new Pontiac front end appeared. It was much more modern looking than before, with the headlamps faired into the front fenders. The design also bridged the styling gap between the earlier models on which it was based and the new generation that would follow. There were new "A" bodies for the renamed entry-level Special Six series. The DeLuxe Six and DeLuxe Eight series used the little-changed GM "B" body. A new Torpedo Eight series used C-body coupe and four-door sedan shells shared with Cadillac, LaSalle, Buick, and Oldsmobile. The grille was evolutionary as well, and the center-oriented vertical-grille design was gone. Pontiac only offered the "woody" station wagon in the Special Six series. It sold for $1015 and came standard with a fender-mounted spare tire.

Now Pontiac takes front rank as the car for those who look ahead!

Today when quality means more than ever Pontiac offers ten new models superior in 15 ways to last year's great success.

Torpedo Business Coupe

Torpedo Sport Coupe

Torpedo Sedan Coupe

Torpedo Two-Door Sedan

Torpedo Four-Door Sedan

Torpedo Metropolitan Four-Door Sedan

Torpedo Convertible Sedan Coupe

ONLY $25 MORE FOR AN EIGHT IN ANY MODEL

Streamliner Sedan Coupe

Streamliner Four-Door Sedan

Pontiac Torpedoes

...With the things you've always liked *and 15 new ones too!*

THIS YEAR YOUR choice of a new car is going to depend—more than ever before—on *how many years it will last.* Because of this, it is more important than ever that you investigate Pontiac before you buy any 1942 car.

The new Pontiacs are improved in 15 ways over last year. They are more beautiful inside and out. Their increased over-all length and weight makes them even more comfortable, without sacrificing any of Pontiac's famous economy. They are still priced just above the lowest-priced cars.

But the really important news is that these new 1942 Pontiacs are *unchanged where quality and long life count most—in pistons, bearings, crankshafts, connecting rods and other vital spots!*

That is why we say the 1942 Pontiac is the perfect car for America today—*and for many years to come!*

GENERAL MOTORS' MASTERPIECE

Full Speed Ahead on National Defense

To the production of a new type of heavy machine gun for the United States Navy, Pontiac is devoting two entire plants, totaling 10 acres of floor space and staffed with thousands of Pontiac production experts and skilled craftsmen working three shifts a day. In addition Pontiac has a total of 223 sub-contractors supplying machines and material to build this new gun which naval authorities describe as "the most effective weapon of its size ever produced." Defense comes first at Pontiac—and Pontiac is going full speed ahead!

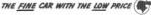

Streamliner Station Wagon

THE _FINE_ CAR WITH THE _LOW_ PRICE

20

1942

TORPEDO SIX

For 1942, Pontiac introduced facelifted styling and shuffled the model lineup from 1941. The slow-selling C-body Custom Torpedo models were discontinued, so Pontiac was down to two platforms. The A-body line was now known solely as Torpedo, and the B-body models were now Streamliners. Additionally, the Super Streamliner subseries was renamed Chieftain to create more distinction between it and its lower-level siblings. On December 7, 1941, the Japanese attack on Pearl Harbor plunged America into World War II. Pontiac continued to build cars, but by December 15 Chieftain production ended and chrome trim was eliminated. The final Streamliner came off the line on February 2, 1942, eight days after Torpedo production ended. Pontiac produced 83,555 cars before the shutdown.

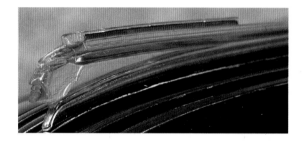

The New PONTIAC... An automobile show all by itself!

The New Pontiac offers GM Hydra-Matic Drive optional* on all models

If you study the illustration above, you will find a car precisely suited to your requirements—for the new Pontiac offers a complete automobile show . . . all by itself! And regardless of the model you select, you may rest assured that it will give you unequalled satisfaction—and unsurpassed economy. For this is the greatest Pontiac ever built.

You can see that it is more beautiful. A few minutes at the wheel will reveal its new brilliance in performance. And the years will prove that even Pontiac's traditional dependability has been enhanced. Truly, it is a fine car made even finer! And, climaxing this great series of improvements, Pontiac now offers General Motors Hydra-Matic Drive as

optional on all fifteen models. Never before has this engineering masterpiece been made available in a car priced so low. So for every reason—from economy to luxury—you should own a Pontiac.

HELP AMERICA PRODUCE FOR PEACE
TURN IN YOUR SCRAP IRON AND STEEL

A fine car made even finer

PONTIAC MOTOR DIVISION of GENERAL MOTORS CORPORATION

IDENTIFICATION OF PONTIAC MODELS AS ILLUSTRATED
GM Hydra-Matic Drive and White Sidewall Tires optional at additional cost.

1948

STREAMLINER SIX

After the war, Pontiac resumed automobile production on September 13, 1945. Other than the return of chrome trim, a new grille, wraparound bumpers, and a few detail changes, the 1946 and 1947 Pontiacs were nearly the same as the 1942 models. It wasn't until 1948 that the prewar design received additional changes, though none were very radical. Visual differences included revised silver streaks, a new grille, round taillight lenses, and the deletion of the "speed ribs" on the fenders. A DeLuxe trim option was available for most models, and cars so equipped included chrome spears on the front fenders. The big news was that GM's Hydra-Matic drive was made optional in Pontiacs, making them the lowest-priced cars available with the revolutionary automatic transmission.

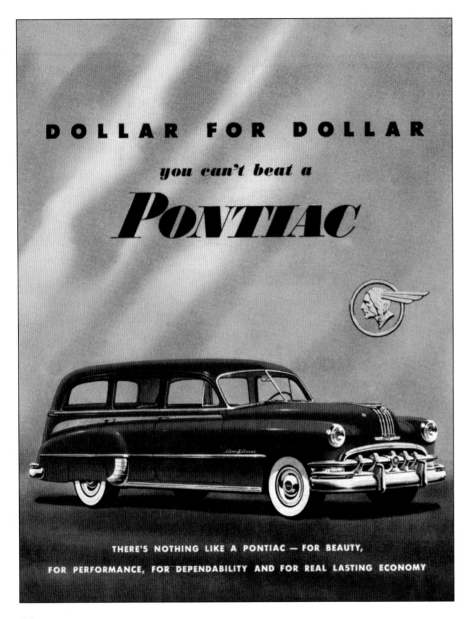

DOLLAR FOR DOLLAR

you can't beat a

PONTIAC

THERE'S NOTHING LIKE A PONTIAC — FOR BEAUTY, FOR PERFORMANCE, FOR DEPENDABILITY AND FOR REAL LASTING ECONOMY

1949

STREAMLINER DᴇLUXE EIGHT

For 1949, Pontiac introduced its first truly new postwar cars. All rode a 120-inch wheelbase, which split the difference between the previous 119- and 122-inch spans. Chieftain notchbacks and Streamliner fastbacks were offered in standard and DeLuxe versions. As before, any Pontiac could be purchased with either a six- or eight-cylinder engine. In addition, either engine could be teamed with Hydra-Matic, now offered at a reduced price of $159. The automatic transmission was increasingly popular; roughly three-quarters of '49 Pontiac buyers chose it. At the beginning of the year, Pontiac wagons still used a small amount of wood in their bodies, but by the time the example shown here was built, steel panels covered with simulated wood replaced the last remaining cabinetwork.

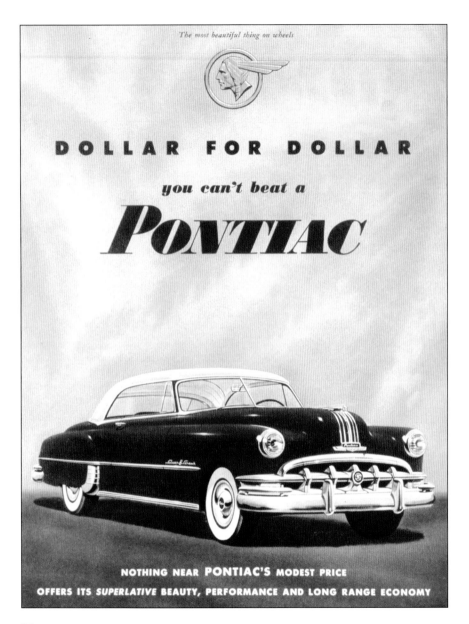

The most beautiful thing on wheels

DOLLAR FOR DOLLAR

you can't beat a

PONTIAC

NOTHING NEAR **PONTIAC'S** MODEST PRICE
OFFERS ITS *SUPERLATIVE* BEAUTY, PERFORMANCE AND LONG RANGE ECONOMY

1950
CHIEFTAIN DeLUXE EIGHT

In introducing its 1950 models, Pontiac basically elected to stand pat with the winning hand it dealt itself in 1949. Styling was virtually unchanged, save for a bolder grille with five prominent vertical bars and a horizontal bar and parking light housings that wrapped around the front fenders. Minor updates included revised hood and decklid emblems and an updated hood ornament. The last could be ordered with Chief Pontiac's face made of plastic instead of chrome, allowing it to light up when the headlights were turned on. Under the hood, the eight-cylinder engine was bored an extra eighth of an inch, raising its displacement from 248.9 to 268.4 cubic inches, boosting horsepower from 103 to 108. An optional high-compression cylinder head raised output to a more robust 113.

DOLLAR FOR DOLLAR YOU CAN'T BEAT A

Pontiac

Equipment, accessories and trim illustrated are subject to change without notice. White sidewall tires at extra cost.

Spectacular—that's the only word for it!

1952

CHIEFTAIN DeLUXE EIGHT

Pontiac dropped the last of the fastback Streamliners during 1951, so when the 1952 models arrived, all were Chieftains including the station wagons and sedan deliveries. There were no sheetmetal changes, but the new models differed visually from the '51s via the grille surround, front nameplate, decklid handle, and—on DeLuxes—the "Dual sweep-spear" bodyside chrome moldings and full disc hubcaps. By this time, 93 percent of Pontiac buyers were opting for the straight-eight engine, and 82 percent chose the automatic transmission. For 1952, the automatic shift was an improved unit called Dual Range Hydra-Matic, which featured four gears and two "high" ranges. As the military action in Korea raged on, government-imposed quotas capped production at lower levels than 1951.

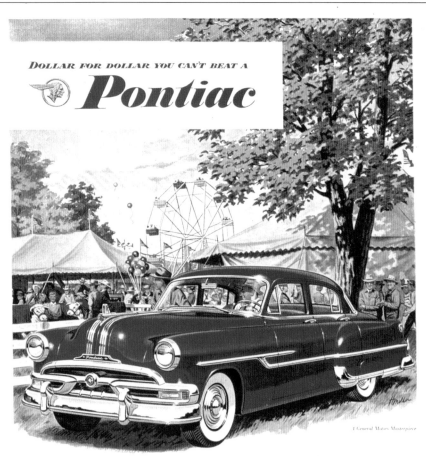

DOLLAR FOR DOLLAR YOU CAN'T BEAT A

Pontiac

Blue Ribbon Winner—in the Dependable Class!

If ribbons were awarded for motor car excellence Pontiac would certainly have a collection second to none!

For Pontiac is obviously a winner when it comes to good looks. There is no car on the road —regardless of price—more instantly recognized and admired than this Silver Streak beauty.

In all-around performance, too, Pontiac is well up in the front rank. Pontiac's great high-com-

pression engine delivers more power than you are ever likely to need. And you get this power with surprising flexibility that insures you of agile performance in traffic and easy-going, economical cruising on the open road.

For solid comfort, for ease of handling, for very high resale value—in fact for all the things which make an automobile great, Pontiac wins top points everywhere, year after year.

But of all its many virtues, the one which most owners think of as Pontiac's blue-ribbon quality is dependability! Pontiac is engineered and built to deliver years and years of wonderful driving with only routine servicing attention.

When you can get all these blue-ribbon qualities at a price just above the very lowest, why should you forego the pleasure of a Pontiac? See your Pontiac dealer and learn how easy it is to own one.

PONTIAC MOTOR DIVISION OF GENERAL MOTORS CORPORATION

1953
CHIEFTAIN EIGHT

By 1953, Pontiac was attempting to shed its stodgy image. New styling on a longer wheelbase helped, but continued use of the familiar flathead engines surely did not. Like Chevrolet, Pontiac adopted new outer sheet-metal and a one-piece curved windshield to give its 1953 models a more "important" look that included vestigial tailfins. Pontiac liked to extol the economic virtues and dependable operation of its Chieftain lineup. The six gained about 15 horsepower this year, so the six- and eight-cylinder engines now differed only slightly in horsepower, but the eight delivered considerably more torque. This was the last year Pontiac offered a sedan delivery in the United States. It was a standard model, but it wore the DeLuxe side trim. Only 1324 of these attractive workhorses were built.

More Style, More Power, And a Built-in Future!

When you buy a Pontiac you make more than a purchase—you make a solid investment in the future.

First of all, Pontiac's years-ahead beauty holds the promise of lasting fashion. And the smart distinction of Pontiac's Twin-Streak styling and Vogue Two-Toning marks you as one of the first to spot a trend.

You make a solid investment, too, in buying the world's most modern power. The smooth, nimble way it glides you through traffic and the instant, surging, passing power it provides on the highway are constant reminders that Pontiac's mighty Strato-Streak V-8 is all that any engine can be.

Your Pontiac investment also pays big dividends in peace of mind and safety. You enjoy handling ease that's still a future goal of many other cars—and you relax in the comfort and solid security of the biggest, huskiest car within hundreds of dollars of Pontiac's price.

Yes, everything about Pontiac says that here's a car that, in a single bold step forward, brings you all that's new and good.

When you consider that you can buy a big, beautiful Pontiac at a price well within any new-car budget, don't you agree that it's the soundest way to invest your automobile dollar? Come in soon for a wonderful buy.

SEE YOUR NEAREST PONTIAC DEALER

Pontiac's Strato-Streak V-8 delivers 200 blazing horsepower with four-barrel carburetor* and is the most modern, most advanced power you can buy. Its entirely new design reflects years of research and development by Pontiac engineers, backed by General Motors' vast technical facilities.

*Low extra-cost option; 180 h.p. standard.

Pontiac

WITH THE SENSATIONAL STRATO-STREAK V-8

1955

STAR CHIEF

Pontiacs were completely redesigned for 1955. The cars still shared the General Motors "A" body with Chevrolet but retained longer wheelbases and specific styling. Also like Chevy, Pontiac boasted a modern V-8 engine for 1955, a 287-cubic-inch "Strato Streak" that replaced all of the old inline engines. The overhead-valve V-8 made up to 180 horsepower in standard form, or 200 with the optional four-barrel carburetor. A column-shift manual gearbox was standard, but nearly 91 percent of '55 Pontiacs left the factory equipped with the Hydra-Matic. The hood carried twin Silver Streaks, and along the crest of each rear fender a Silver Streak curved down to emphasize the tail lamp. The Star Chief convertible shown here was the glamour barge of the line.

32

It's The Talk of the Test Drivers!

THIS FABULOUS '56 PONTIAC WITH THE BIG AND VITAL GENERAL MOTORS "AUTOMOTIVE FIRST"!

Ever try to impress a test driver? Believe us—it isn't easy!

So — we're tremendously proud to report that the '56 Pontiac has these thrill-wise experts cheering. They're excited in a really big way about its fabulous new performance.

What's set them buzzing is the very thing that will put a new lilt in your days when you come in and take the wheel—that big and vital General Motors "First" combining:

Pontiac's new, big-bore Strato-Streak V-8 with the terrific thrust of 227 blazing horsepower.

General Motors' new, fluid-flow Strato-Flight Hydra-Matic* that gentles this mighty "go" to smoothness beyond belief.

In all truth, here is the lift of a lifetime for all in love with great performance. And you don't need a test track to prove it!

Traffic will tell you. Here's "stop-and-go" response that matches the speed of your thoughts. *A hill will help.* High or low, it's left behind without a sign of effort. *And passing definitely pins it down.* Gun it and instant, buoyant power sweeps you smoothly past the loitering truck ahead. No drag, no lag—just safe and certain "go"!

A few miles of this and you're ready to join the club. For this is living as you've never lived on wheels before!

To be sure, there's more to charm you in this glamorous '56 Pontiac. The safety of big, authoritative new brakes. The security of finer control, sure-footed cornering, a super-steady new ride. New beauty and luxury that brilliantly mirror tomorrow.

But, above all, it's the fabulous "go" that gets you!

Come in and drive a Pontiac soon for a glorious double thrill. There'll be pride in your heart, a torrent at your toe-tip. And what more could anyone want? *An extra cost option.*

SEE YOUR NEAREST PONTIAC DEALER

'56 **PONTIAC**

1956
CHIEFTAIN 870

More chrome and cubic inches highlighted numerous updates for 1956 Pontiacs. All models now packed a "Strato-Streak" V-8 enlarged to 317 cubic inches. Horsepower ran from 192 to a hot version with twin four-barrel carburetors that was rated at 285. This year Pontiac offered the Chieftain "860" base and "870" midline series and top-of-the-line Star Chiefs including the spectacular two-door Safari wagon. As they had in 1955, Chieftains ran a 122-inch wheelbase and Star Chiefs, save the Safari, used a 124-inch span. Pontiac joined the industry swing to four-door hardtops by adding a stylish Catalina to each of the three series. In late summer, the 6-millionth Pontiac was built, a Star Chief Custom Catalina hardtop coupe.

1957
BONNEVILLE

Semon E. "Bunkie" Knudsen became Pontiac's general manager on July 1, 1956, and he was determined to create a younger image for the brand. Quickly, he ordered the removal of the Silver Streaks from the hood of the 1957 Pontiac. Then the limited production Bonneville convertible arrived. Built on the Star Chief's 124-inch wheelbase, the image-building Bonneville was the plushest, most powerful Pontiac to that point. Under the hood was an exclusive 370-cubic-inch V-8 engine that was equipped with mechanical fuel injection and was good for 310 horsepower. Specific side trim helped set the Bonneville apart from lesser Pontiac drop tops, as did the long list of standard equipment. The hefty $5782 price was enough to buy a Star Chief convertible and a Super Chief sedan with $7 to spare.

1957
STAR CHIEF SAFARI

Effective with the introduction of the 1957 models, all Pontiac station wagons bore the Safari name. The moniker debuted in 1955 on a high-style two-door wagon that shared bodies with Chevrolet's Nomad. The special two-door (right) appeared for the last time in 1957, when only 1292 were built. Although aficionados tend to think of that two-door as the "true" Safari, the four-door Transcontinental (left) strutted its own unique features. The most obvious was the side trim: anodized aluminum on the rear doors and quarter panels riding beneath a modified spear. Within the straightened spear were four chrome stars (the two-door Safari got only three), followed by Safari script. Special paint colors and a roof rack were standard, as was leather upholstery. Production came to 1984 units.

LOW PRICE CAR
WITH
HIGH PRICE LOOKS
...AND ACTION!

Size it up! This big, bold Pontiac Chieftain has a brand of beauty, luxury and performance *completely new* to the low-price field! It's man-size in every dimension with a road-hugging 122-inch wheelbase! And, inside, more space and elegance than you've ever known at anywhere near the price; with high-fashion fabrics, an incredible array of color choices, and the luxury bonus of wall-to-wall carpeting *even in the lowest priced model!*

Try it out! Big as it is, the Chieftain handles like a feather—functions with an effortless drill team precision that will positively amaze you! And it's no wonder, for here are literally dozens of innovations, ranging from a suspension system that virtually eliminates dive, sway and bounce . . . to the Tempest 395 engine, Pontiac's brilliant new power plant that is tooled to tolerances finer than the finest watches—to bring you a new jeweled-action smoothness in motion!

Compare the cost! See your Pontiac dealer and take a moment to prove what thousands of Chieftain owners already know: *Pontiac beats the best of the low-price three —and does it for less money!*

PONTIAC MOTOR DIVISION OF GENERAL MOTORS CORPORATION

The Golden Jubilee Car

BIG BOLD PONTIAC

A BOLD NEW CAR FOR A BOLD NEW GENERATION

40

1958
CHIEFTAIN CATALINA

The 1958 Pontiacs received a total make-
over with longer and lower new bodies, but
wheelbases stood pat despite a redesigned
X-brace chassis. Pontiac's fresh quad-
headlight front end took center stage, but
also new was the line-wide application of the
370-cubic-inch V-8 previously seen only in the
Bonneville. The 370 was good for 240 to 300
horsepower, or 310 in fuel-injected Bonneville
guise. Bonneville remained atop the lineup,
but a two-door hardtop with a unique body
was added to the existing convertible. The
ragtop saw a monumental $2200 price cut
to $3586, and the hardtop listed for $3481.
In Pontiac's entry-level Chieftain series, a
sharp Catalina two-door hardtop like the one
shown here cost $2707. Though less lavish
than upper models, Chieftains were gener-
ously chromed.

Pontiac surrounds a man with beauty
and the solid security of wide-track wheels

We've been noticing something interesting about our men customers. When a man becomes the owner of a 1959 Pontiac he slices a few years off his age, becomes enthusiastic about driving almost anywhere any time, and holds his head a bit higher, a lot more proudly. It's not our imagination. It actually happens.

Unofficial psychology explains it this way: A man who works hard and gives his all to profession and family has earned the right to drive a great automobile. A Wide-Track Pontiac is a perfect reward.

Its trim, sleek lines gratify your sense of good taste and refinement. Yet they're well-defined lines, positive but uncluttered, consistent and clean. The

unique grille is a good example; different but highly imaginative and pleasing.

Man is born to be a master and Pontiac gives you masterful control of this car with the security and stability of Wide-Track Wheels; wheels moved five inches farther apart. This widens the stance, not the car. You're balanced, with less lean and sway.

We assure all well-deserving men that this automobile will give you a vigorously fresh outlook on life, a feeling of youth, accomplishment and much, much pride. Show your wife this advertisement; she deserves a Pontiac, too.

PONTIAC MOTOR DIVISION · GENERAL MOTORS CORPORATION

THE ONLY CAR WITH WIDE-TRACK WHEELS

Dotted lines show conventional wheel positions. Pontiac's wheels are five inches farther apart. This widens the stance, not the car. Pontiac hugs tighter on curves and corners. Sway and lean are considerably reduced, ride is smoother, balanced, steadier.

YOU GET THE SOLID QUALITY OF BODY BY FISHER.

PONTIAC! America's Number ① Road Car!

3 Totally New Series · Catalina · Star Chief · Bonneville

1959
BONNEVILLE SAFARI

For 1959, Pontiac adopted a completely new identity. "Wide Track," a twin-nacelle grille, and a new arrow-point badge became principal Pontiac hallmarks. They persisted through the Sixties and Seventies, and the split grille and arrow point signified Pontiacs until the marque's end. Even though there was a new body for 1958, all 1959 General Motors cars were again outfitted with new bodies, in response to Chrysler Corporation's radical 1957 designs. From an engineering standpoint, the big differences in 1959 were the Wide Track suspension that moved the wheels out closer to the body sheetmetal and the addition of the 389-cubic-inch V-8. Pontiacs came in three series: Catalina, Star Chief, and Bonneville. The Bonneville line added a four-door Vista hardtop sedan and a Custom Safari wagon.

you get a
fresh point of view
...from Pontiac!

The Bonneville Sports Coupe for 1960

The precision control of Wide-Track Wheels!
The smoothness of supple suspension!
The resourceful energy of Tempest V-8 Engines!

You find it attractive because of the delightful absence of over-design.

You're drawn to its crisp freedom, its perfect form, its exhilarating freshness.

You'll find it amiably obedient because of Wide-Track Wheels and an ingenious suspension system. Wide-Track firms the foundation, stabilizes, balances. A softer suspension makes it responsive, quick and easy to take direction.

Pontiac's Tempest engines for 1960 are more vigorous than ever. You have a wide choice of V-8 power packages, ranging from the high performance 425 to the economical 425E which prefers regular grade gasoline.

The people of the Pontiac Motor Division are never content with the commonplace, never hemmed in by the hackneyed. This is why you will receive a delightfully fresh point of view from the ownership of a 1960 Pontiac.

The car, the keys, the catalog, the courtesy—all await you at your Pontiac dealer.

PONTIAC MOTOR DIVISION • GENERAL MOTORS CORPORATION

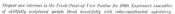

NARROW TRACK
PONTIAC'S WIDE-TRACK

Wider stance gives you swayless stability, solid comfort. You maneuver with skillful sureness, accurate control. It's the most rewarding driving you've ever felt!

PONTIAC
THE ONLY CAR WITH WIDE·TRACK WHEELS

44

1960
BONNEVILLE

The 1960 Pontiacs sold even better than the all-new '59s on which they were based. A new Ventura series, fresh styling from the beltline down, and new colors aided the cause. As did the continued promotion of Wide Track design that genuinely enhanced the appearance of all Pontiacs. All '60 Ponchos used a 389-cubic-inch V-8, which ranged from an economical 215 horsepower job up to the 348-horse Tri-Power monster. With their classy dashboards and multitoned "Morrokide" upholstery, Pontiac interiors were some of the most dazzling of the day. The Vista Sedan four-door hardtop (right), a body style that debuted for 1959, was again the most popular Bonneville model with 39,037 sold. The unique wraparound rear window design was shared with other GM four-door hardtops.

Why a Wide-Track Pontiac delivers you fresh and ready for fun

There's a remarkable absence of "fatigue factors" in this refreshing car.

Front and rear suspension systems have been specially tailored for Wide-Track. This creates a ride as smooth as a tide-washed beach. Quietness and cornering control are improved.

More durable, rubber-insulated body mounts are used to keep road hum down where only the tires can hear it. Extra body insulation and sealing eliminate

tiring noise and vibration for near-perfect acoustics.

New Wide-Track design contributes to greater stability. More weight is balanced between the wheels. You feel an invigorating response, unwavering control.

Next time you feel like going places, let the tireless Pontiac spirit move you. It's the awakening, Wide-Track way to travel that starts at your fine Pontiac dealer's. Visit him soon and take that deciding drive.

PONTIAC MOTOR DIVISION · GENERAL MOTORS CORPORATION

THE ONLY WIDE-TRACK CAR
Pontiac has the widest track of any car. Body width trimmed to reduce side overhang. More weight balanced between the wheels for sure-footed driving stability.

IT'S ALL PONTIAC! ON A NEW WIDE-TRACK!

1961
VENTURA

Pontiac's redesigned fleet of big cars for 1961 revived the split-grille theme on shorter and lower but roomier bodies. Fifties favorites, such as fins and chrome, were toned down for a cleaner look. Bonneville returned as the top model on a new 123-inch-wheelbase chassis that it shared with the Star Chief. Catalina and the tonier Ventura shared a new 119-inch span, as did Bonneville wagons. All big Pontiacs used the 389-cubic-inch V-8, which could be ordered with as much as 348 horsepower. Late in the year, a special-order 421-cube Super Duty engine with 373 horsepower debuted. Pontiac was carefully cultivating a performance image, and the new lighter cars and more powerful engines made Pontiacs tough to beat on the street or the race track.

"Pontiac's Tempest is the CAR OF THE YEAR" .. Motor Trend
says it, Tempest owners agree!   Gas-saving 4-cylinder engine •
110-155 h.p. front engine/rear transmission • independent 4-wheel suspension

1961
TEMPEST

Pontiac's interpretation of GM's new compact trio looked conventional on the outside and echoed the big car's styling, down to the split grille. Beneath the skin, Tempest went its own way. While the related Buick and Oldsmobile compacts used only a new 215-cubic-inch V-8, Pontiac used half of a 389 V-8 to create a 195-cubic-inch inline four that went into about 98 percent of Tempests; the balance received the 215 V-8. Both engines linked to a rear-mounted transaxle via a flexible drive-shaft that ran inside of a torque tube. Front suspension was independent, and swing axles made the rear independent too. Tempest initially came as a four-door sedan or wagon; a two-door coupe was added during the year. Production came to 100,783 units, easily out-pacing its corporate cousins.

How to stop staring at other people's Pontiacs

Put yourself in an easy-to-own Catalina. It's "Cat" quick and crisply styled. Longer, lower and loaded with the brand of gumption that has made Pontiac the one to watch and want. Trophy V-8 Engine ratings from 215 to 348. Turning radius shortened as much as 3½ feet to end "jockeying" in tight spots. Smart new interiors—fully carpeted and finely appointed. Wide-Track balance that keeps roads of all kinds under control. Why not start Wide-Tracking yourself! It couldn't be easier than in this Catalina. Check one out today at your Pontiac dealer's.

Wide-Track Pontiac CATALINA • STAR CHIEF • BONNEVILLE • GRAND PRIX

1962
BONNEVILLE

Nineteen sixty-two was a breakthrough year for Pontiac, when more than a half-million of the division's products were built, including more than 380,000 full-size models. This astounding leap made Pontiac third in industry production for the first time. Styling was evolutionary, with the now-expected "beak" serving to split a grille of horizontal bars. C-shaped taillights wrapped around the rear cove, and rooflines were shuffled. Two-door hardtops adopted a faux convertible look, while sedans did away with the last vestige of the "back porch" design first seen on the '59s. The Ventura disappeared as a series but lived on as a custom interior package for Catalina hardtops. Catalinas rode a 120-inch wheelbase, with the Star Chiefs and Bonnevilles using a 123-inch span.

This beauty eats mountains for breakfast—Pontiac Grand Prix! Point the G.P. uphill, and you find its 303 h.p. Trophy V-8 flattens towering grades almost casually. (And by paying a bit more, you can pick from engines ranging way on up in horsepower.) The custom-styled G.P. doesn't just look like a finely honed piece of road machinery—it is, in fact, the real article. Let's tick off some of the reasons: Deep-cradling bucket seats, center console with tach, plus floor-mounted Hydra-Matic and four-speed stick as extra-cost options. And the G.P., you'll be happy to know, has Pontiac's road-wedded Wide-Track. See your Pontiac dealer—the G.P. man. Pontiac Motor Division, General Motors Corporation.

GP Grand Prix

1962
GRAND PRIX

The Grand Prix was the flagship of the 1962 Pontiac line. Based on the Catalina hardtop coupe, Grand Prix was fitted with a sports-car-oriented interior and wore cleaned-up styling. Although the GP used no unique body panels, the exterior was marked by sparingly applied brightwork. It also sported a revised grille, grillework in the rear cove between the taillights, and exclusive rocker panel trim. Grand Prix badges adorned the front and rear grilles as well as the recessed sculptures in the doors. All in all, the GP stood out as a masterpiece of understatement. Inside, bucket seats were upholstered in Morrokide, a material with the look and feel of leather. With a base price of $3490, the Grand Prix didn't come cheap, but dealers managed to move 30,195 copies.

It may be some time before you can see this car without a lot of people crowded around it —so be our guest. In all good conscience, we can't let you rush off buying a Grand Prix without letting you in on what's under that beautiful skin. For one thing, a thoroughly well-mannered Trophy V-8 of 303 horsepower (on up to 370 hp at extra cost). For two things, a pair of the handsomest, most comfortable seats this side of your living room. Self-adjusting brakes. Even, at modest extra cost, a steering wheel that you can adjust to fit your style of driving (or your size). And a host of things mechanical that'll keep your GP strong longer. So you see? You can buy one for purely rational reasons—if you really want to. The man to see is your Pontiac dealer. He's the Keeper of the Wide-Tracks.

PONTIAC GRAND PRIX

1963
CATALINA

Youthful and energetic, Pontiac's 1963 restyle was one of the era's benchmarks. The full-size model's stacked headlights would be copied by other makers. The Grand Prix entered its sophomore season wearing handsome new sheetmetal with smooth bodysides, a concave rear window, and "hidden" taillights. Most of this look carried over to the rest of the Pontiac line, save for the GP's roofline and details. Catalinas were dressed up with a simple spear down the length of the flat bodysides. Star Chiefs added to that a stack of stylized stars on the roof sail panels. On Bonnevilles, a thick, ribbed trim piece projected back from the headlight bezels to about the middle of the front doors. On all, the a-pillars now ran straight through the cowl. Model year production set a new record at 590,071.

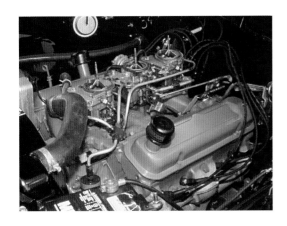

meet Tempest '63...today!

how's this for exploding the myth that cars have to be expensive to look it! Tempest '63

Maybe you can tell the difference between Pontiac's Tempest (especially that Le Mans) and the high-priced jobs. Besides the four that acts like a V-8, Tempest now offers a 260-hp V-8* that acts like nothing you ever drove. And besides its beautiful balance, Tempest sports a Wide-Track this year. And self-adjusting brakes and a tach* and clean, fresh styling. About all it doesn't have is a big fat price tag. But who cares? **Pontiac Tempest**

*Optional at extra cost.   Pontiac Motor Division · General Motors Corporation

1963
TEMPEST

The 1963 model year was one of sweeping and significant changes to Pontiac's senior compact. All-new sheetmetal below the belt-line gave Tempest a more upscale look. The body was a bit more slab-sided, with noticeably longer rear quarters that contributed to an additional five inches of length. Under the hood, the four-cylinder engine was reworked a bit, and the optional 215-cube aluminum V-8 was history. In its place was a small-bore version of the cast-iron 389 displacing 326 cubic inches. The automatic transmission was revised, and the rear suspension was changed from the swing-axle arrangement used in 1961 and '62, to a new trailing arm design. The ritzier LeMans coupe and convertible became a separate series and LeMans was positioned more upscale as a kind of junior Grand Prix.

We don't have to spend time telling people how beautiful Pontiac is. People tell us.

For that matter, the only people we ever have to talk to are people who've never driven a Pontiac. After you've sampled Wide-Track stability and Trophy V-8 action, what's left to say? After you've enjoyed Pontiac's silent, smooth ride, who needs more convincing? Frankly, about all we can say is that a Pontiac is a whole lot more car than other cars that think they're the competition. And your Pontiac dealer can show you *that* with great ease. '64 WIDE-TRACK PONTIAC

PONTIAC MOTOR DIVISION • GENERAL MOTORS CORPORATION

1964
BONNEVILLE

For '64, big Pontiacs got terrific new styling with stacked headlamps and a clean tail. The model offerings remained constant, but Pontiac created a new 2+2 option group for Catalina convertibles and two-door hardtops. Included were the obligatory bucket seats and console and 2+2 badging. The package cost $291 and drew 7998 orders. A slightly revised lineup of eight 389-cubic-inch engines began with an optional 230-horsepower "economy" engine for automatic-transmission equipped cars to an available 330-horse Tri-Power unit. Also 421 V-8s were available with up to 370 horses. The new LeMans GTO would soon redefine the performance car, but for now hot models were still specially equipped large cars. All told, Pontiac remained the third-best selling automotive brand.

PONTIAC MOTOR DIVISION • GENERAL MOTORS CORPORATION

Don't let the Pontiac style, the Pontiac performance, and the Pontiac quality fool you —Tempest is a low-priced car.

It's a little difficult convincing some people that you can't tell a Tempest by its price tag. Especially people who've been buying the same old low-priced make time after time.

This Tempest of ours, you see, looks and feels and performs like it should carry a positively awesome figure. That's because of its longer, roomier body, wider Wide-Track, bigger brakes, rugged new frame, even the new 140-hp 6. You've got seven models to choose from, but don't fret about making the choice. After all, they're all designed by Pontiac. How could anybody go wrong? **WIDE-TRACK PONTIAC TEMPEST**

1964
TEMPEST GTO

For 1964, Tempest shelved its transaxle design for GM's conventional new intermediate chassis, then set the automotive world afire with the GTO. The Tempest GTO was the first modern mass-produced automobile to put big-cube power in a midsize body—the formula that defined the true muscle car. To do this, Pontiac circumvented a GM rule that forbid intermediates from having V-8s over 330 cubic inches by including the 389 V-8 as part of an option package, a ploy that didn't require corporate approval. GTO's magic was being the first "factory hot rod" marketed as an integrated performance package, with a key component being a carefully cultivated image. But GTO had the goods, starting with at least 325 horsepower. Pontiac hoped to sell 5000 GTOs in 1964, but the tally was 32,450.

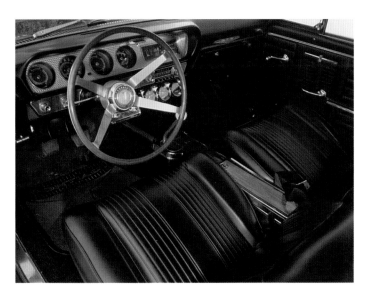

Women like Pontiacs just for their looks.

Men like Pontiacs just for their liveliness.

Who's kidding who?

Women like beauty, men crave action. But something like Pontiac can bring them together. Sure, men love the performance of that 389-cubic inch engine (even more when it's teamed with the smoothness of optional Turbo Hydra-Matic), but so do their mates. Women exclaim over the sleek exterior styling and the luxury interior, but men are quick to second the motion. And the matchless stability and handling of Pontiac's Wide-Track stance cuts across all lines—everybody loves it. So what have we done? We've engineered a temporary truce in the Battle of the Sexes. **Pontiac '65/Year of the Quick Wide-Tracks.**

1965
CATALINA

Pontiac's renaissance was in full swing by 1965. The division's full-size cars were redesigned on a new chassis. The styling used the marque's familiar design cues—split grilles, stacked headlamps, slotted taillamps, etc.— and brought them to a whole new level. In particular, the bodysides were a fairly radical departure from previous editions in that they featured a more exaggerated "Coke-bottle" shape than before. The full-size line consisted of Catalina, Grand Prix, and wagons on a 121-inch wheelbase, and Star Chief and Bonneville on a 124-inch span. Ventura and 2+2 packages were offered on certain Catalina models, and a Brougham group could be ordered on the Bonneville four-door hardtop. The year's most popular full-size Pontiac was the Catalina two-door hardtop (right).

1965
TEMPEST GTO

For 1965, the intermediate-size Tempest and LeMans received a handsome facelift with vertical headlamps, crisper styling, and three more inches of length. Offerings came in Tempest, Tempest Custom, and Tempest Le-Mans series. The trendsetting GTO returned as a $296 option package for LeMans Sport Coupes, hardtops, and convertibles. GTO kept its 389-cube V-8, but the base version gained 10 horsepower to 335. The optional Tri-Power unit was good for 360. GTO sales more than doubled to 75,352, nearly a quarter of the Tempest production run. The stylish two-door hardtop was available in the Tempest Custom series for the first time (left), but nearly three times as many buyers spent an extra $145 to get the tonier LeMans trim.

Don't make any snap decisions on buying our new Executive.

Wait until you've seen our other 39 models.

It won't be easy. Even for Pontiac, Star Chief Executive is one mean achievement: big-car looks, big-car ride, little-car price. 124-inch Bonneville chassis, 389-cubic inch V-8, interiors that make you think a spoiled potentate had the last word, backup lights for better visibility in night maneuvers to the rear. All in one package priced low enough to make a lot of lesser cars hide in shame. A unique personality. But the point is that our other 39 models have personalities equally unique, equally exciting. You name your kind of car and we've got it. From the super-luxurious Brougham in 3 models, to the all-new Tempest with the unique overhead cam engine. And if we've talked you into looking over all 40 of our tigers, don't be ungrateful. At least we've confined your new-car hunting to one showroom. **WIDE-TRACK PONTIAC/'66**

1966
CATALINA

Pontiac's full-size lineup was shuffled a bit for 1966. Tweaks included the replacement of Star Chief with the Star Chief Executive, the 2+2 became a separate series, and wagons shed the Safari label. A handsome facelift included a new grille design. Most models retained the center beak and grilles divided by a horizontal bar. In 1965, the treatment was rigidly horizontal, but for '66 the stylists drew up grille halves that narrowed as they neared the center of the car. Also new was a frenched treatment for the stacked head-lamps. Out back, fresh touches included the taillamps and the panel that housed them, along with blade-like caps for the ends of the fenders. Catalinas sold the best, and with production of 80,483, the bread-and-butter four-door sedan (right) was most popular.

1966 Pontiac Grand Prix.   Who said you can't buy success?

Grand Prix's secret, like all successes, is that there's nothing else quite like it. An elegant driving machine. Elegance that begins with an arrogantly sculptured body and ends with a surfeit of accommodations: Stráto bucket seats, center console, flexible assist bar, silent electric clock, walnut-trimmed instrument panel and steering wheel—even dual-speed wipers with washers to clear your way ahead. The flip side of the Grand Prix sales record is a stable of V-8's of up to 376 hp, capable of bringing every nuance of the sporting Wide-Track suspension into vivid reality. Enough driving excitement to make you wonder why the kids haven't caught onto it yet. If you're after luxury with a kick, get inside a Grand Prix. You'll still find it only at your Pontiac dealer's.

GM

1966
GRAND PRIX

Pontiac's entry in the growing "personal luxury" field continued to be the Grand Prix hardtop coupe, which was built on the Catalina chassis but featured distinct grille, roof, and rear styling. The Grand Prix's grille used an open design without the horizontal divider, and the turn signals were again set in the grille openings. The result meant the GP looked much like a big brother to the GTO. Out back, there was an exclusive rear-end design with a quartet of thin horizontal strips that ran the width of the tail panel and hid the taillamps when they were not illuminated. Also new was the ribbed bright trim under the sculpture line on the lower bodysides. This was a big car that tipped the scales at 4015 pounds and started at $3492. The handsome eight-lug wheels were optional for about $130.

Does anything this sleek and luxurious really need a revolutionary new overhead cam six? No. We just like it better that way.

Pontiac Motor Division • General Motors Corporation

Wide-Track Pontiac/'66

1966
GTO

Youthful and aggressive, Pontiac's revamp of its midsize line was among the decade's best styling jobs. The redesigned bodies with their "Coke-bottle" shape were particularly handsome in two-door form. In a day of V-8 dominance, Pontiac released a sophisticated overhead-cam inline six-cylinder engine. The 230-cubic-inch engine was rated at 165 horsepower and was standard in the Tempest and LeMans. With the 4-barrel Sprint option, it was good for 207 ponies. A 6000-rpm redline gave the six a European feel. The GTO became a separate model line this year and sold 96,946 copies, the highest ever one-year total for a true muscle car. Pillared coupes, hardtops, and convertibles were offered, all with a 389-cube V-8; the 360-horse version was good for 0-60 mph in 6.5 seconds.

It looks like a lot more people will be driving station wagons this year.

That tastefully sculpted Executive Safari you see up there is bound to change a lot of thinking about station wagons. Along with its equally new Tempest Safari cousin, it was designed to prove that a wagon can look as good at the opera as it does out at Lake Winnebago. Together, they bring to eight the number of Pontiac wagons designed for everything from seeing America first to delivering Junior and seven friends to PS 32.

Our new 400 cubic inch V-8 is Executive's standard moving force (our revolutionary Over-head Cam 6 powers the Tempest series) and a flock of new options like a stereo tape player are available to help make getting there more than half the fun.

To get you there safely, we've added new safety features like folding seat back latches, a four-way hazard warning flasher and General Motors' new energy absorbing steering column. Your Pontiac dealer has the whole story. Just tell him you want to get out of town. In style.

Pontiac 67/Ride the Wide-Track Winning Streak

1967
BONNEVILLE

Pontiac marked its sixth year as Detroit's third-best seller in 1967. This season, GM's full-size fleet was restyled. At Pontiac, this meant wedge-shape front fender tips, a low, heavy-looking bumper grille, and a return to creased lower flanks. Wheelbases stood pat at 121 inches for Catalinas and all wagons, with Executives (the Star Chief part of the moniker was retired for '67) and Bonnevilles at 124. Full-size Pontiacs now came standard with a 400-cubic-inch V-8 under the hood; 428-cube versions were optional. This year, Pontiac only put the Safari nameplate on wagons with simulated woodgrain panels. In the full-size line, the label only appeared on the new Executive Safari in six- and nine-passenger versions.

1967
GRAND PRIX

Perhaps the most surprising Grand Prix news for 1967 was the introduction of the first—and as matters developed, the last—Grand Prix convertible. Listing at $3813, it cost $264 more than the hardtop and enjoyed a modest production run of 5856 units. Styling changes on the reskinned Grand Prix were extensive. The headlamps were now hidden under the outer ends of the horizontal-bar grille, and the parking lights were behind three horizontal slits at the top of the front fenders. Taillamps were unique per Grand Prix tradition, and both bodystyles featured hidden windshield wipers, an industry first. In another change, the vent windows were eliminated on the hardtop. The base engine was now 350-horsepower 400-cubic-inch V-8. Optional mills were limited to 360- and 376-horse 428s.

The Great Pontiac, showing the hood-mounted tachometer option. Naturally, we make a handbrake and a bootle inside, too. All have a host of standard safety features that just a few things we've mentioned.

GM

Pontiac Motor Division

The Great One is here.

This incredibly sleek mass is the 1967 Pontiac GTO. At rest. Four hundred cubic inches of engine under a magnificently refined new skin. In 255 and 335 horsepower variations. With even more of the distinguishing features that have made The Great One great. You can order things like our new 360-hp Quadra-Power 400, a 3-speed Turbo Hydra-Matic with manual shift control, front wheel disc brakes, eight-track stereo. Nor have we neglected its understudies—LeMans and Tempest. The 165-hp Overhead Cam Six is standard. A 215-hp OHC 6 (with or without the Sprint option) is available, as are 250- and 285-hp V-8s. New interiors. New colors. New options. New safety features, like a dual master cylinder brake system with warning light. And the road-hugging security of Wide-Track. 1967 may now begin. **Pontiac 67/Ride the Wide-Track winning streak**

1967

GTO

GTO was back, stylish as ever for 1967. The dazzling 1966 look was updated with a "chain-link" grille and a resclupted tail with "lid-less" taillamps. Under the hood, the 389 was bored out to 400 cubes, and three flavors were on the menu. The base engine ran a Quadrajet carb and was good for 335 horsepower. An optional High Output four-barrel version replaced the discontinued Tri-Power setup and was good for 360 ponies. The Ram Air mill was also rated at 360 horses. Ram Air included a functional hood scoop, plus a pan that surrounded the open-element air cleaner and mated to the hood with a foam skirt. Increased competition ate into GTO sales, but production was still a healthy 81,722 units. The pillared Sports Coupe started at $2871, the hardtop at $2935, and the ragtop at $3165.

You'd expect Pontiac
to come up with a nifty new sports car like this.

Firebird Sprint

Firebird

Firebird HO

Firebird 326

Firebird 400

But did you expect five?

When you think about it, no single sports car can satisfy everybody. We thought about it. So now you have five choices. All excellent.

You say you want an economical fun car? Try *Firebird*, and swing with our regular-gas 165-hp Overhead Cam Six. You say you lean toward a family sportster? Lean on *Firebird 326* and you'll be moved by a 326 cubic inch V-8 that delivers 250 hp (yes, 250!) on regular.

Ah, you say, but the real you is a European-style road machine. Good. That's why we invented *Firebird Sprint*: special suspension, 3-speed floor shift and a 215-hp version of the Overhead Cam. Our light heavyweight is entitled *Firebird HO*. It entitles you to things like dual exhausts, sports striping and a potent 285-hp V-8. And if you're looking for the ultimate in heroic driving, you'll find it in *Firebird 400*, with 400 cubes of chromed V-8 that put out 325 hp with no sweat.

All share the same superb styling and interiors. And, of course, all come with the complete GM safety package. You say you're glad we think of everybody? Somebody has to.

GM
MARK OF EXCELLENCE

The Magnificent Five are here!

1967
FIREBIRD

Pontiac entered the ponycar market with the 1967 Firebird. Closely related to corporate cousin Chevy's Camaro, Pontiac's "F-body" offering used the same 108-inch wheelbase, separate front subframe, and unit-body construction. Firebird was sold in five flavors: base, Sprint, 326 V-8, HO, and 400. Base and Sprint used Pontiac's 230-cubic-inch overhead-cam inline six (165 and 215 horsepower). The V-8 models used the 326 in two forms: two-barrel with 250 horses, and the four-barrel HO with an honest 285 ponies. The most exciting model came with the 400 V-8 from the '67 GTO. Firebird 400 packed 325 horsepower under its twin-scooped hood. Firebird production started in January 1967 at the Norwood, Ohio, plant. Total hardtop and convertible production was 82,558 units.

A Wide-Track luxury car with dual exhausts, buckets and console-mounted shifter can't be called ordinary. We call it Grand Prix.

Many of today's cars are tagged with names that lead one to expect greatness at every turn. But, much to the chagrin of the buyer, the great things remain just that: expectation. One exception, however, is Grand Prix. This machine is everything, if not more, that its nomenclature conjures in the mind of the beholder.

Pop open its hood, and you're staring at the Grand Prix's standard, 400-cubic-inch, 350-hp, 4-barrel V-8. To command this magnificent combination of cubes, carb and cam, an all-synchro 3-speed Hurst shifter—floor-mounted, of course. And for a finishing touch, be sure to observe those dual exhausts that make that big, smooth V-8 even smoother.

But we did call Grand Prix a luxury car, didn't we? And one look at those long, sweeping lines above gives you a hint of the opulence within. Opulence in the form of Carpathian burled elm vinyl on the doors. And more of the same on the dash, where there's a place for everything, and everything is in its place.

So if you've had your fill of ordinary, may we suggest Wide-Tracking? All it takes is one visit to your Pontiac dealer's. And two words: Grand Prix. Follow those directions, and ordinary will become a thing of the past.

Pontiac Motor Division

Wide-Track 1968 Pontiacs

1968
CATALINA

Full-size Pontiacs for 1968 wore horizontal headlamps located inside a huge bumper/grille with a prominent vertical center bulge. Catalinas, the Grand Prix two-door hardtop, and all wagons rode a 121-inch wheelbase, while the remaining Executives and Bonnevilles used a 3-inch-longer span. A 400-cubic-inch V-8 was standard in each, but horsepower ratings ranged from 290 in Catalinas and Executives to 350 in the GP. The top engine option was a 390-horse 428. The Catalina range offered the widest selection of body styles, including a price leader two-door sedan that started at $2945 (right). It didn't prove popular though, with only 5247 sold. The Grand Prix had a heavy new look that must have left some buyers cold because the model's sales fell by more than a quarter to 31,711.

We've just received our 4th Car of the Year award. But with a car like this, what did you expect?

Below, the 1968 GTO, better known as The Great One. It's this year's recipient of Motor Trend magazine's Car of the Year award. Which means that Pontiac now has the distinction of being the only car manufacturer in the world to have won this award four separate times.

The award was given for the engineering of the whole car. The most significant feature of which is a revolutionary bumper that's so fantastic you have to kick it to believe it. This amazing super-snout is not only the same lustrous color as the car, but it won't chip, fade or corrode.

But don't get the impression that The Great One is all show. With a 400-cubic-inch, 4-barrel V-8 or our Ram Air engine with deep-breathing scoops, the GTO is Wide-Tracking at its ultimate. With all this going for The Great One, did you really have any doubts about which car is this year's Car of the Year?

Of course not. Maybe that's because everything our engineers touch turns to great.

You can also enjoy America's fastest growing sport in our other fantastic '68 Pontiacs, including LeMans, Tempest Custom and Tempest.   Pontiac Motor Division

Wide-Track 1968 Pontiacs

1968
GTO

The first all-new GTO since 1964 was introduced for '68. The sleek new body rested on a shorter 112-inch wheelbase, and the curvaceous lines were highlighted by a revolutionary body-colored "Endura" front bumper that gave a little on impact. Hidden headlamps were so popular on the new "Goat" that most people didn't realize they were an option. Under the hood, the familiar Pontiac V-8s returned. The standard 400-cubic-inch V-8 was rated at 350 horsepower, the next step up was the 360-horse H.O. that came with Ram Air. Midyear, the Ram Air II was introduced, with round exhaust ports and a new camshaft. Playing it cool, Pontiac rated its hottest GTO engine at the same 360 ponies. The new model proved popular with performance lovers, and sales were up slightly to 87,684 units.

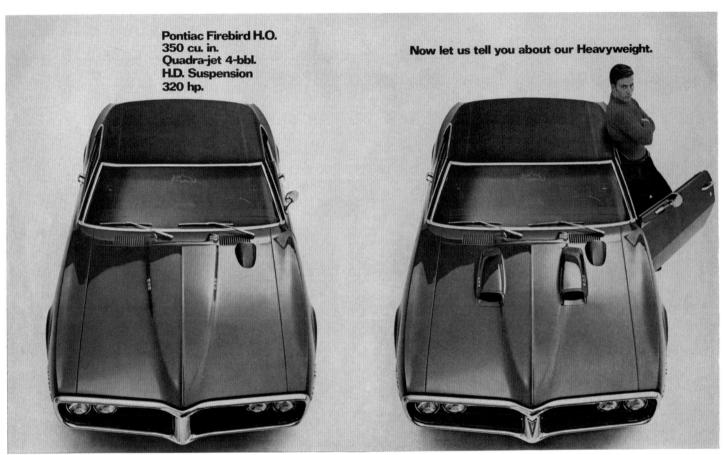

**Pontiac Firebird H.O.
350 cu. in.
Quadra-jet 4-bbl.
H.D. Suspension
320 hp.**

Now let us tell you about our Heavyweight.

You see it on the right. Our 400. Heavyweight of Pontiac's Magnificent Five Firebirds for 1968.

Along with its heavy-duty but newly obliging suspension (asymmetrically mounted multiple leaf rear springs and wide-ovals) there's a heavy-duty 3-speed with Hurst shifter. All standard. And augmented by a 330-hp, 400-cu.-in. V-8 with 430 ft. lbs. of torque and Quadra-jet. Or you can select the new 335-hp H.O. engine, or a 335-hp Ram Air with functional scoops.

But don't think we'd surround you with all that exuberance and neglect elegance. Any Firebird can be ordered with knitted (just like mom used to make) vinyl upholstery. And picture windows (no side vents), carpeting, and simulated wood grain styling on dash are standard. And with every Firebird you get GM's many safety features. Like seat belts, safety armrests, and side-mounted marker lights.

Now, any guess why we decided to call them the Magnificent Five—again?

Pontiac Motor Division

1968
FIREBIRD

Firebird lost its vent windows for 1968 but otherwise was little changed save for shuffled engine choices. The base overhead-cam six gained 20 cubic inches (to 250), which boosted horsepower to 175. With the optional four-barrel, output jumped to 215. Spicing up the six didn't impress buyers, however, as the vast majority of '68 Firebirds got one of the optional V-8s. The new 350-cubic-inch jobs that replaced the 326 were especially popular. The optional hood-mounted tachometer looked neat but was hard to read in rain or snow or with bright sun at your back. As on other 1968 Pontiacs, Firebirds satisfied the U.S. government's newly mandated sidemarker-light regulations by adding an illuminated red Pontiac "arrowhead" badge on each rear fender. Production climbed to 107,112 units.

1969
CATALINA

For 1969, Pontiac's full-size cars were redesigned, but they looked similar to the '68s. Catalinas and station wagons rode a 122-inch wheelbase, while Executives and Bonnevilles used a 125-inch span—both one inch longer than before. Catalinas and Executives had a 290-horsepower 400-cubic-inch V-8 standard, but buyers could choose a 265-horse version that ran on regular gas instead. Bonnevilles used a 400 that was good for 360 ponies; it was optional on other full-size Pontiacs. Catalinas came in a full array of body styles including a four-door sedan, two- and four-door hardtops, six- and nine-passenger wagons, and a convertible. The drop-top Catalina started at $3476, but only 5436 were ordered. The Bonneville convertible listed for $3896 and outsold its sibling by a mere two units.

What if Pontiac decided to build a car like this? Pontiac decided.

Leaving competition in the lurch is a way of life to Pontiac's ingenious engineers. And the swank Pontiac Grand Prix parked on this page ought to tell you they're living up to their image. Our '69 Grand Prix is so new, in fact, it's based on its very own, one-of-a-kind chassis that rides like it was designed for cruising, but built for cornering. That swooping hood (over six feet long, we hasten to add) covers an equally impressive department: 350 hp is standard, or you can order up to a 390-hp V-8. Floor-mounted, 3-speed stick is standard, but there's always the super-slick, 3-speed Turbo Hydra-matic, if you want to order it. There's also an interior that suggests interplanetary travel, and the only other thing we can say about it is that it's also available in leather. As for the Grand Prix radio antenna: Ask your Pontiac dealer. He's the man to let you in on the automotive secret of the year.

'69—The year of the great Pontiac break away

GM MARK OF EXCELLENCE

The Wide-Track Family for '69: Grand Prix, Bonneville, Brougham, Executive, Catalina, GTO, LeMans, Custom S, Tempest and Firebird. Pontiac Motor Division

1969
GRAND PRIX

Bucking an industry trend, the redesigned 1969 Grand Prix shrunk three inches in wheelbase (to 118 inches) and lost 360 pounds (now 3715). Yet, this trimmer GP sported one of the longest hoods in autodom. With 400- and 428-cubic-inch V-8s with up to 390 horsepower available, the Grand Prix combined muscle-car go with luxury car comfort. As per tradition, there was one body style, a $3866 two-door hardtop. Standard equipment included the industry's first concealed radio antenna that was embedded in the windshield and an aircraft-style cockpit with Strato-bucket seats. A GTO-inspired hood-mounted tachometer was optional. The new Grand Prix was a very attractive package, and buyers stepped up and took delivery of 112,486 copies; more than triple 1968's tally.

89

1969
LeMANS SPRINT

It may seem like it today, but back in 1969 all midsize Pontiacs were not GTOs. This year, Pontiac also offered Tempest, Custom S, and LeMans models. These "A-body" cars used dual wheelbases: 116 inches on four doors and wagons, and 112 inches on two doors and convertibles. The cheapest models were the Tempests, in pillared two-door Sports Coupe and four-door sedan form. Custom S added two-door hardtop, convertible, and station wagon styles. The top-line LeMans came in two- and four-door hardtop, ragtop, and wood-trimmed Safari wagon form. This Le-Mans convertible has the Sprint package that was optional on any of these models, save the wagons. It added a 4-barrel carb to the OHC six, a floor-shifted 3-speed stick, heavy-duty shocks, sway bar, and bodyside stripes.

Pontiac Motor Division

Born great.

Did you expect less? Shame! This is The Judge. And The Judge claims Pontiac's great GTO as its closest of kin.

Which explains The Judge's bump-proof Endura snoot. And the bulging hood scoops which can be opened or closed from the driver's seat. And the very unspongy springs and shocks. And the Morrokide-covered front buckets. And the no-nonsense instrument panel.

Now, if you want to think of The Judge as Billy's kid brother, OK. Just keep in mind that the family resemblance only goes so far.

You see, The Judge comes on with a 60″ air foil. A custom grille. Big, black fiber glass belted tires. Special mag-type wheels. Blue-red-yellow striping. And name tags (like the wild one below) inside and out.

Keep in mind also that this baby performs like nobody's kid brother. Not with a standard 366-hp, 400-cube V-8 and Ram Air. Or a 370-horse Ram Air IV, if you so order. Either couples to a fully synchronized 3-speed with a Hurst shifter. Or order a close-ratio 4-speed. (Little old ladies might even order Turbo Hydra-matic.)

No sir. The kid brother hasn't been born yet that's greater, or tougher than The Judge.

THE JUDGE A SPECIAL GTO BY PONTIAC

Four color pictures, specs, book jackets and decals are yours for 30¢ (50¢ outside U.S.A.). Write to: '69 Wide-Tracks, P.O. Box 888B, 196 Wide-Track Blvd., Pontiac, Michigan 48056.

1969
GTO JUDGE

"The Great One" got minor styling updates and a whimsical new performance model for 1969. Pontiac added op-art decals, a rear spoiler, and a 366-horsepower Ram Air III 400-cube V-8 to create the Judge, as a $332 option package for the GTO hardtop and convertible. The car's name was a sly pop-culture reference—"Here come da Judge" was a recurring catchphrase on the TV show *Laugh-In*. The first 5000 Judges were painted Carousel Red (a bright shade of orange), but other colors were offered later in the model year. Options included the underrated 370-horse Ram Air IV engine, a close-ratio four-speed or automatic transmissions, Posi, front discs, power steering, and a hood-mounted tach. Judge production for '69 was 6725 hardtops and 108 convertibles.

Firebird Trans Am.

Back when the Chisholm Trail was this country's idea of an expressway, you needed 335 horses to haul the mail. We figure you still do. So Firebird Trans Am's got 'em. Stabled under oversized hood scoops in 400 cubic inches of Ram Air V-8. A heavy-duty, 3-speed, fully synchronized manual transmission helps you hitch them to a 3.55:1 rear axle and F70—14 fiber-glass-belted tires. Wells Fargo rides again!

Now before you get the idea that Trans Am is strictly for wide open spaces, take it through a mountain pass. Standard heavy-duty shocks, heavy-duty springs, 1" stabilizer bar, power front disc brakes and variable-ratio power steering make Trans Am our version of the quarter horse.

But you can probably guess all that by looking at it. Trans Am's engine air exhaust louvers, rear-deck airfoil, black-textured grille, full-length blue stripes and special I.D. provide fair warning that this is no ordinary mount. It's Pontiac's new pony express. And that's just a little this side of air mail.

Four color pictures, specs, book jackets and decals are yours for 30¢ (50¢ outside U.S.A.). Write to: '69 Wide-Tracks, P.O. Box 888F, 196 Wide-Track Blvd., Pontiac, Michigan 48056.

GM

MARK OF EXCELLENCE

Pontiac Motor Division

1969
FIREBIRD 400

The 1969 Firebirds wore new sheetmetal as well as revised front and rear styling. In March 1969, Pontiac unleashed the $725 Trans Am Performance and Appearance package with little fanfare. To the Firebird it added a functional twin-scoop hood, rear spoiler, open front fender vents, and a unique white and blue paint scheme. Trans Am production was limited to 697 coupes and eight convertibles. Firebird engine choices included 175- and 230-horsepower versions of the 250-cubic-inch overhead-cam inline six, and 350- and 400-cube V-8s. The top engine option for both Firebird 400 HOs and Trans Ams was the 345-horsepower Ram Air IV 400. A four-speed came with the Ram Air IV, and a three-speed automatic was optional. Sales slumped to 75,362 coupes and 11,649 ragtops.

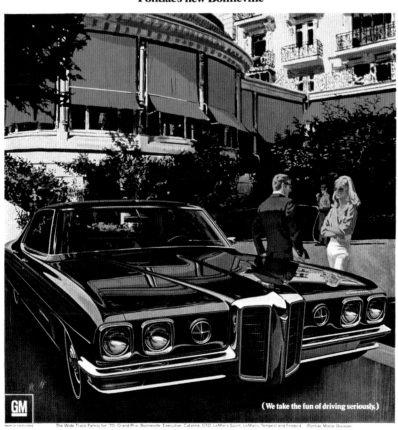

It takes a Pontiac to change your ideas about luxury.

Pontiac's new Bonneville is here. With more sheer styling excitement in its classic nose than most cars have in their entire bodies.

But we wouldn't want you to settle for beauty alone. We didn't. Which explains the standard 360-horsepower, 455-cubic-inch V-8. The comfortably solid Wide-Track ride. The long-wearing, fiberglass-belted tires. The protective steel beams in the doors. Not to mention an interior endowed with the richest patterned fabrics in Pontiac history.

One thing more. Bonneville's fun to drive. Try it. At your Pontiac dealer's. It's the way luxury is going to be.

Pontiac's new Bonneville

GM

(We take the fun of driving seriously.)

The Wide-Track Family for '70: Grand Prix, Bonneville, Executive, Catalina, GTO, LeMans Sport, LeMans, Tempest and Firebird. Pontiac Motor Division.

1970
CATALINA

Pontiac had become a sales force to be reckoned with during the Sixties with bold, exciting cars. By 1970, that boldness was exemplified in its large cars. Unfortunately for Pontiac, big and brawny was beginning to fall out of favor, and sales would suffer. The face of the 1970 full-sized Pontiacs harked back to the classic era with a narrow vertical grille and a thin biplane-style bumper. Low-line Catalinas and all wagons rode a 122-inch wheelbase, with Executives and Bonnevilles on a 125-inch span. Pontiac's former 428-cubic-inch V-8 was bored and stroked to become a 455 for 1970. Standard in Bonnevilles and optional in the other full sizers, the new top-dog V-8 came in 360- and 370-horse flavors. The Catalina convertible started at $3604; only 3686 were made.

(We take the fun of driving seriously.)

GM
MARK OF EXCELLENCE

Pontiac Motor Division

The quick way out of the minor leagues

Every year, Pontiac gets tougher on upstarts.
Not that we go out of our way to discourage amateur performers. We just take the fun of driving very seriously.
Like engines. GTO's standard is a 350-horsepower V-8. But this year there's a high-torque 455-cu.-in. V-8 to order, as well as two Ram Airs. So someone's bound to get his feelings hurt. Letting you order a new, low-restriction exhaust should be the final blow.
Sorry, men. But this is the major league. And it's time to make a cut.

Pontiac's new GTO.

1970
GTO JUDGE

Pontiac altered the GTO's styling for 1970, giving it a new Endura nose with exposed headlamps, sharp bodyside creases, and a revised rump. Underhood, a newly optional 360-horsepower 455 V-8 provided 500 lb-ft of torque at just 3100 rpm, perfect for the option-laden luxury tourers many Goats had become. Pontiac kept the Judge focused on performance, so the 455 was kept off the docket until the last quarter of the model year. Most Judges packed the 366-horse 400-cube Ram Air III mill, but a handful had the extra-cost Ram Air IV with 370 ponies. Few cars made a bolder visual statement. "The Judge" decals returned, multi-hued stripes appeared over the bodyside creases, and the 60-inch rear wing now stood high and proud on the tail.

(We take the fun of driving seriously.)

Any licensed driver is eligible to participate.

In the beginning of tomorrow. Which is where it's at when you take your seat in the 1970 Firebird Trans Am.

The stick is from Hurst. And it controls a wide-ratio 4-speed transmission. Just right for making the 400 Ram Air V-8 do what you want it to.

You'll know exactly what it's doing, too. Thanks to the tach, speedometer, voltmeter and oil, water and fuel gauges set in that engine-turned aluminum instrument panel.

The thick wheel is our 14" Formula version. It goes directly to the extra-quick, variable-ratio power steering. You have to feel it to believe it.

Outside, the Trans Am is all function. An air dam under the Endura bumper and a spoiler at each wheel will help keep the car aerodynamically stable. Cooling air, that goes to the engine, is vented through two side air extractors. Preventing air buildup in the engine compartment. All these

good things are standard. And combined with the rear spoiler, they create a downward pressure of 50 lbs., both front and rear. At turnpike speeds.

Trans Am. It's our ultimate Firebird.

The Firebird Formula 400 is enough to be anyone else's ultimate car. It develops 430 lb-ft of torque from the standard 400 V-8. Order Ram Air, and those twin fiberglass scoops allow cold air to be rammed into the four-barrel carburetor.

Like every Firebird, the Formula 400 has front bucket seats. Bucket-type seats in the rear. Front *and* rear stabilizer bars help give a flatter ride.

Trans Am or Formula 400. Only Pontiac could build them. So naturally they're only at your Pontiac dealer's. Better get over there. If you want in on the beginning of tomorrow.

Firebird. New, even for Pontiac.

1970
FIREBIRD FORMULA 400

Firebird grew more European in nature with the second-generation redesign that appeared in late February 1970, but the scooped and spoilered Trans Am was pure American muscle, and more immodest than ever. Functional spoilers and vents abounded, while super-tough underpinnings and quickened steering gave it corner-hungry handling. Only the strongest 400-cubic-inch V-8s were offered; a 345-horsepower Ram Air was standard, while a 375-horse Ram Air IV was optional. The Firebird Formula 400 shed the Trans Am's spoilers and swapped out the "shaker" hood for a twin-scooped fiberglass unit. It came with a 330-horse 400, and the scoops were functional when Ram Air was ordered. The new Firebirds were all slippery fastbacks; a convertible was not available.

The first
Grand Ville

If anybody could introduce a true luxury car with a sensible price, Pontiac could.

Twice the money won't buy a smoother ride.

Traditionally, elite cars come expensive. But Pontiac never regards tradition as sacred. Not even when it comes to building a luxury car like our first Grand Ville. Which doesn't come expensive.

Pontiac's smoothest, quietest ride ever.
All Pontiacs are known for a smooth Wide-Track ride. But in the Grand Ville, we labored long and hard to find new ways to marry the body to the chassis. And it paid off. Grand Ville has an unbelievably luxurious ride.

The formal roofline does more than attract oohs and aahs.
It makes Grand Ville the most spacious Pontiac. With extra head and shoulder room. The Grand Ville 2-door Hardtop also has as much rear-seat leg room as most people's 4-doors.

Rich. Richer. Richest.
Grand Ville's upholstery depends on the model you order. But they're all very rich. Right up to an exclusive brocade that comes with the custom interior available.

Even the performance is luxurious.
Variable-ratio power steering is standard. Power brakes (discs up front), standard. A 455-cubic-inch V-8, standard. And like all Pontiac engines for 1971, it's designed to operate efficiently on the new low-lead or no-lead gasolines. With lower exhaust emissions.

Extra protection built in.
Everything that looks like painted metal around the grille and headlamps isn't metal at all. It's a tough Pontiac material that resists dents and dings.
As in all Pontiacs, you also enjoy extra security from such safety features as side-guard beams in the doors and an energy absorbing steering column.

One more time on the price.
If you agree that Grand Ville's an impressive automobile, you won't object to a reminder that it's sensibly priced. Because that makes our Grand Ville worth consideration. And you can consider now. At your Pontiac dealer's.

Pure Pontiac!

1971
GRAND VILLE

Pontiac had an all-new series of big cars for 1971. Catalina was still the low-end model, but Bonneville was demoted to mid-line status. The top-of-the-line series for '71 was the Grand Ville. The Grand Ville—offered in two- and four-door hardtop styles, along with a convertible—was the closest Pontiac would ever get to having GM's prestigious "C" body return to its lineup. Based on the "B" body, Grand Villes borrowed formal hardtop rooflines from the new C-body Cadillac, Buick Electra, and Oldsmobile Ninety-Eight. This clever parts swapping gave Pontiac a new premium series and kept costs manageable. Grand Villes used the four-barrel version of the 455 that was optional on the other full-size models. The $4706 Grand Ville convertible sold 1789 copies.

There's a little GTO in every GT-37.
And you don't have to be over 30 to afford it!

It's Pure Pontiac!

1971
LeMANS SPORT

Pontiac's midsize line was facelifted for 1971, and the Tempest name was retired. The base car was called T-37, then came LeMans, Le-Mans Sport, and GTO in ascending order. All wore restyled front ends, and the GTO also benefited from a new hood. When equipped with one of the optional V-8 engines, the T-37 coupe and hardtop coupe models could be turned into a GT-37, kind of a budget GTO. GT-37 equipment included dual exhausts, floor-mounted heavy-duty three-speed manual transmission, Judge-style Rally II wheels with G70-14 white-letter tires, hood pins, vinyl body stripes, and specific badging. LeMans Sport models, like the convertible shown, were available with an Endura styling option that added the new GTO body-color front bumper, hood, and headlamp assemblies.

1972 Pontiac Grand Prix. You'll have to decide what's better...the style or the ride.

It won't be easy. After all, the styling is timeless. Enduring. While the ride is definitely Wide-Track. Smooth. Stable. With great handling.

If making a decision seems difficult, it's even tougher should you include Grand Prix's unique interior design in the mixture.

It's functional. The instrument panel has a wraparound shape that makes gauge-reading and switch-flipping unusually easy.

Yet it's elegant. Foam-padded bucket or bench seats in Morrokide or cloth trimmed in Morrokide. Carpeting. Console with the bucket seats. Cushioned steering wheel. And more.

You'll also find Pontiac innovation in Grand Prix. Windshield radio antenna. Concealed wipers. Power-Flex fan. And on the available Grand Prix SJ model, a Delco-X battery that never needs water.

There's amazing response built into the drive train and suspension. You get a 400 V-8 standard (a 455 V-8 is available). Variable-ratio power steering, standard. Power brakes with front discs and rear drums, standard. And smooth Turbo Hydra-matic transmission, also standard.

Now if it seems like you're getting a lot of car in Grand Prix, you haven't seen anything yet. Because Grand Prix has a long list of safety features. Energy-absorbing steering column. Seat and shoulder belts. Front-seat head restraints. Dual master cylinder brake system with warning light. And headlamp aiming access provision.

As you can see, when you try to decide what's better (or best) about the 1972 Grand Prix—style, ride, design innovation, performance or the standard safety equipment—it's quite a choice.

But then, maybe that's what makes Grand Prix so interesting to drive.

Don't forget to buckle up for safety.

That's what keeps Pontiac a cut above.

GM
MARK OF EXCELLENCE
Pontiac Motor Division

1972

GRAND PRIX HURST SSJ

The popular Grand Prix was updated for 1971 with new styling at each end. Up front, the vertical grille wasn't as pointed as it was in 1969 and '70, and two headlamps replaced four. Out back, a boattail-style rear deck was adopted. For 1972, GP was largely the same, but a fresh grille texture, a maintenance-free battery, and a handful of tweaks gave Pontiac salesmen a few talking points. Of particular interest was the limited-production Hurst SSJ Grand Prix that was first offered in 1970. The conversion took place in a Hurst facility and was based on a Cameo White or Starlight Black Model J. For $1147, special touches included Hurst's distinctive Firefrost Gold paint on the hood, roof, rear deck, and the Rally II wheels, a landau-style vinyl top, and an electrically operated steel sunroof.

All the luxury you want without buying more car than you need. 1972 Luxury LeMans by Pontiac.

Time was, the only way to get a truly luxurious automobile was to buy big. Luxury, so it seemed, was in direct ratio to length of wheelbase.

No more. Now if you want luxury, there's a new mid-sized Pontiac that should fit you perfectly.

It's called Luxury LeMans. And it beautifully illustrates why luxury doesn't have to be measured by the running foot.

On the outside, Luxury LeMans offers uncommon mid-sized luxury, via a distinctive new grille, deluxe wheel covers, rear-wheel fender skirts and the liberal (but not heavy-handed) addition of bright metal trim.

The interior further proves that full-sized cars don't have an exclusive on luxury. There's plush carpet. Yards of it, even clear up the lower door panels.

There's an instrument panel with the look of rare Ceylonese teak. A squeez-able steering wheel that fits your hands as if it were cast for them. And more soundproofing throughout to help make our new Luxury LeMans the quietest mid-sized Pontiac ever.

Yet with all this, we think the best example of Luxury LeMans' elegance is the seating. Inches of soft foam pad-ding. Rich fabrics. And vinyls so soft they warrant a tanner's hallmark. Quite frankly, you'd be hard put to find comparable seating in some limousines.

Now, we want you to enjoy all this luxury. So Luxury LeMans—like other 1972 Pontiacs—includes a long list of safety features. Padded instrument panel, energy-absorbing steering column, front-seat head restraints, Side-guard steel door beams and many more.

So, look. If you're thinking of a lux-ury car this year (and want one that's easy to park and economical to operate), slip into the new '72 Luxury LeMans.

You'll discover it at your Pontiac dealer's now.

Don't forget to buckle up for safety.

That's what keeps Pontiac a cut above.

1972
GTO

Industry wide, performance wasn't selling the way it had only a few years earlier. Personal luxury was sought by more and more buyers, so Pontiac added the Luxury LeMans to its midsize lineup. Luxury LeMans came as two- and four-door hardtops. Exterior differences included a specific grille, trim, wheel covers, rear fender skirts, and badges. Interior upgrades included simulated Ceylonese teak trim, extra sound insulation, and all-Morrokide or patterned cloth and Morrokide upholstery. On the other end of the midsize Pontiac spectrum, the GTO was now a $344 option package for two-door LeMans coupes and hardtops. The little-ordered Judge and convertible were quietly retired. GTO appearance was little changed, but a revised grille and front-fender vents were new.

Introducing the first Grand Am. From Pontiac, of course.

GRAND AM has the feel of a Grand Prix...the response of a GTO... the characteristics you've admired in fine road cars.

Let's say you've always driven American cars... always been intrigued with imports. Perhaps you've envied the handling...or the real wood in the interior. Whatever.

We think you'll find our first Grand Am a more-than-acceptable alternative.

The suspension was designed for the steel-belted, wide-base radial tires. With thick front and rear stabilizer bars for precise cornering.

Grand Am responds with a 400 V-8 and 3-speed Turbo Hydra-matic. Power front disc brakes and fast, variable-ratio power steering are standard.

Pontiac's been known for bumpers since '68. But Grand Am's new front bumper system is special even for us. And everything around the bumper that looks like sheet metal is really squeezable stuff that gives and springs back.

The Grand Prix feeling is inside. African crossfire mahogany on the instrument panel. Rally instrumentation. Wide-wale corduroy or all-Morrokide upholstery on special deep-contoured seats.

Special because the front buckets recline. And they have adjustable lower back supports. Also special because we put them in a 4-door, as well as a 2-door.

Sound like your kind of car? Better find our kind of dealer. Pontiac, of course.

1973
GTO

The once mighty GTO was fading by 1973. It remained an option package for the redesigned base and Sport LeMans coupe. Despite an included 400-cubic-inch V-8 and heavy-duty three-speed floorshift transmission, it was less convincing than GTOs of just a few years before. The only visual distinctions from its LeMans brothers included a NACA-scooped hood, black grilles, and specific badging. Pontiac's big news on the midsize front was the new Grand Am, clearly related to the LeMans and its ilk but different enough to merit separate-series status. The basic idea of this coupe and sedan was Grand Prix comfort and luxury with Firebird Trans Am handling. Critics hailed it as the best-handling Detroit car of its time, but the public bought only about 43,000 copies.

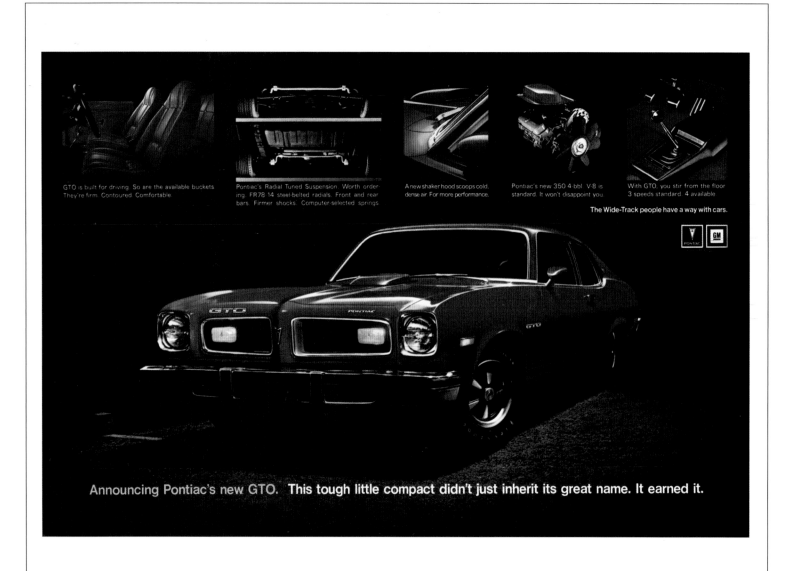

GTO is built for driving. So are the available buckets. They're firm. Contoured. Comfortable.

Pontiac's Radial Tuned Suspension. Worth ordering. FR78-14 steel-belted radials. Front and rear bars. Firmer shocks. Computer-selected springs.

A new shaker hood scoops cold, dense air. For more performance.

Pontiac's new 350 4-bbl. V-8 is standard. It won't disappoint you.

With GTO, you stir from the floor. 3 speeds standard. 4 available.

The Wide-Track people have a way with cars.

Announcing Pontiac's new GTO. This tough little compact didn't just inherit its great name. It earned it.

1974
GTO

The name was the same, but the image, and most of the performance, was gone. Based on the ho-hum Ventura compact—a Chevrolet Nova clone—the GTO was a mere shadow of itself by 1974. Two pillared coupe body styles were available: One had a traditional trunk, and the other came with a hatchback that opened up to a cargo area that could be enlarged by folding down the rear seat. Only 7058 were built with the $195 GTO option package, which included a distinctive grille, "shaker" hood scoop, and a 350-cubic-inch V-8 rated at 200 horsepower. Purists bemoaned the 1974s, recalling the days when the GTO stood for driving excitement. The designation vanished into Pontiac history after 1974 until it reappeared in 2004 on a muscular coupe that was built by General Motors in Australia.

1974 Pontiac Firebirds.

Part engineering.
Part soul.

There's something about a 1974 Firebird you won't find in any fact sheet or spec book.

Because it's something you can't weigh or measure or touch. It's something you have to feel.

We call it soul.

Take the '74 Formula Firebird for example. Any spec sheet will tell you it comes with a 350, 400 or 455 V-8. A floor-shifted 3-speed trans. Performance dual exhausts. Hood scoops. Front disc brakes. And front and rear stabilizers. A very impressive list of features.

But no feature list can explain what it's like to drive a Formula 'Bird. Gauges set so you can read them at a glance. Controls positioned so they seem like they're extensions of your arms and legs. Response so quick it almost anticipates your commands. And an overall driving experience that makes it hard to suppress a toothy grin.

That's the soul of a Firebird.

The '74 Firebird Trans Am is even better. Because what we know about performance driving, we make standard on Trans Am.

A 400 4-bbl. V-8. 4-speed trans. Power front disc brakes. A limited-slip axle. Full instrumentation. F60—15 tires on 7" Rally II wheels.

A shaker hood. A complete entourage of functional air dams, extractors, deflectors and spoilers.

And enough soul to make Trans Am the ultimate Firebird.

Anybody can appreciate Firebird's engineering. To appreciate the soul, you have to love driving cars as much as we love building them.

Pontiac Motor Division

The Wide-Track people have a way with cars.

1974

FIREBIRD TRANS AM

For 1974, Pontiac's Firebird was deftly restyled to accommodate the new federal "crash bumpers" without ruffling its great-looking feathers. The much-needed facelift added a "shovel-nose" Endura front end with Pontiac's traditional split grille, and larger taillights. Base, Esprit, Formula, and Trans Am models were available. The big news on the power front was a rollback for the Trans Am. The standard V-8 became a 225-horsepower 400-cubic-inch job, and a Super Duty 455 with 290 ponies was optional. The later is a rare bird, appearing in only 943 cars, just 212 of them with stick shift. Sales spurted upward in 1974, a bit surprising in light of higher fuel prices resulting from the Arab oil embargo. A total of 73,729 Firebirds were built, including a record 10,225 Trans Ams.

1975
GRAND VILLE BROUGHAM

Pontiac's full-size line evolved a bit every year during the first half of the Seventies, and the constant tweaking kept the cars fresh. Visual changes for 1975 included new rooflines for nearly all the closed models other than the station wagons. Rectangular quad head-lamps, a new trend for upper-level GM cars, were found on Bonnevilles and Grand Villes. In addition, the 1975 model year proved to be significant for a few reasons. It marked the debut of catalytic converters in most models to further reduce exhaust emissions. These new devices required the use of unleaded fuel to avoid damage to their internal compo-nents. Also, the convertible body style made its final appearance in Pontiac's full-size line, when a total of 4519 Grand Ville Brougham droptops were sold.

WHAT PRICE GREATNESS? $5,109.*

A remarkably reasonable price for Pontiac's beautiful new 1977 Grand Prix.

For the timelessness of Grand Prix's styling. The clean, uncluttered lines. The classic profile. The look that continues to elude Grand Prix's imitators.

A surprisingly affordable price for Grand Prix's celebrated comforts. The deep foam seating. The rich fabrics and carpet. The new luxury cushion steering wheel. And the wraparound instrument panel with electric clock. All standard.

A very appealing price for Grand Prix's famed responsiveness.

Variable ratio power steering. Power front disc brakes. Turbo Hydra-matic. Radial Tuned Suspension with steel-belted radial tires. And Pontiac's new 5.0-litre (301-CID) 2-bbl. V-8.* An exciting new design from the Wide-Track people. All standard.

An absolutely beautiful price for a car that is inspiring legends. And one that can make you something of a legend yourself.

Buy or lease a new 1977 Pontiac.

*Manufacturer's suggested retail price including dealer preparation. State and local taxes, destination charges and available equipment additional (bucket seats $141.00, body-colored Rally II wheels $106.00, whitewall tires $43.00, body-colored sport mirrors $31.00, upright front bumper guards $19.00 and painted body stripes $43.00).

See your California or high altitude county Pontiac dealer for applicable power trains and prices.

*Not available in California and high altitude counties.

1977 GRAND PRIX BY PONTIAC ▽ THE MARK OF GREAT CARS

1977
GRAND PRIX

Like all GM intermediates, Pontiac's Grand Prix was redesigned for 1973. The basic body was shared with Chevrolet, Oldsmobile, and Buick, and the wheelbase shrunk two inches to 116. Luxury coupes were extremely popular during the mid and late Seventies, and Grand Prix was no exception, finding more than 288,000 buyers in 1977. This was the best year ever for GP sales, and the last year before the car was dramatically downsized for 1978. This season all three trim levels—base, SJ, and LJ—enjoyed full model status. The base car (right) was the most popular model with 168,247 assembles. The standard engine was a new 301-cubic-inch Pontiac V-8 that was good for 135 horsepower. The fancy LJ started at $5753, but the bottom line could top $9000 if every option was ordered.

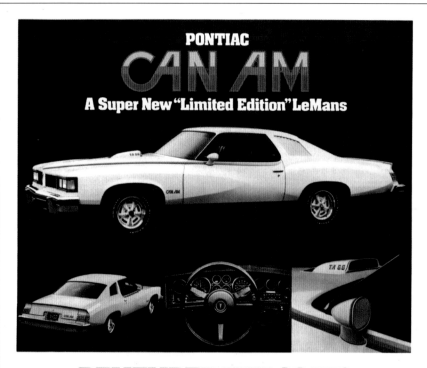

Check out CAN AM'S credentials (they're all standard)

New T/A 6.6 litre (400 CID) 4-bbl. V-8—*Just like the TRANS-AM* (Not available in California and high altitude counties. 6.6 litre (403 CID) 4-bbl. V-8 available in California and high altitude counties, only.

Trans-Am Type "Shaker" Hood Scoop—*That really shakes*

Contoured Rear Deck Spoiler

Tri-Tone Accent Stripes and Tri-Tone CAN AM I.D. (inside and out)

Grand Prix Instrument Panel (shown here with optional Custom Sports steering wheel)

Rally Handling Package with H.D. Stabilizers, front and rear

GR70 x 15 Steel-belted Radials on body color Rally II Wheels

Twin Sport Mirrors

And, of course, Power Steering, Power Front Disc/Rear Drum Brakes and Heavy Duty Turbo Hydra-matic. It's available at your Pontiac dealer now.

GM

CAN AM BY PONTIAC ▼ THE MARK OF GREAT CARS

1977

CAN AM

Nineteen seventy-seven was a few years after the last GTO but just before Pontiac's intermediates would be downsized. It was in between fuel crises. In this tiny peephole of opportunity, Pontiac reinjected some performance into its LeMans. Starting with a LeMans Sport Coupe, engineers mixed in beefier running gear and the Trans Am's 200-horse 400 V-8 (California and high-altitude cars had an Oldsmobile-sourced 403 with 185 ponies), a "shaker" hood scoop, rear spoiler, and decals. Also included in the $5419 base price were power front brakes, variable ratio power steering, front and rear stabilizers, and Pontiac's RTS handling package teamed with GR70-15 steel-belted radial tires. All wore Cameo White paint with red/orange/yellow trim and a Grand Prix-style dash.

Whoever said America's love affair with cars is over has obviously never driven a Pontiac Firebird.

Now in its eleventh year, this great American sport continues to turn casual drivers into raving enthusiasts.

Whether it's the lowest-priced Firebird. The super plush Firebird Esprit. The racy Formula. Or our ultimate sport, Firebird Trans Am. The reaction's the same.

And speaking of Trans Am, just looking at it is enough to make your goose bumps rise. That aggressive new blacked-out grille. All those air dams, spoilers, extractors and deflectors. On our special-edition model, you can even order a sky-opening hatch roof with removable panels.

The excitement builds as you lift the new shaker hood. Because Trans Am sports a bold 6.6 litre 4-bbl. V-8. And if you're looking for something more, there's the available new T/A 6.6.* It has the horsepower of last year's 455 V-8 over a broader rpm range.

But what really hooks you is when you open the door. You sit back in deep-contoured Morrokide or newly available velour cloth bucket seats.

You look over a gleaming machine-turned dash with full rally gauges, clock and tachometer. You get a grip on a thickly padded Formula steering wheel.

You turn the key. And suddenly, you discover the moves that have made Trans Am one of the most popular road cars built in America.

Trans Am. One of four great Firebirds to get enthused about for 1977. See them all.

For over a decade, Firebird's been turning drivers into enthusiasts.

1977

FIREBIRD TRANS AM

Pontiac stylists were nothing if not clever. They had the ability to periodically impart a refreshing new look on the Firebird without serious modifications to the sheetmetal. This year buyers were offered a pointed snout with quad headlights set in a split grille. The 455 passed after 1976, leaving a 400-cube V-8 for the Trans Am—unless you lived in California or at high altitude where a Olds-built 403 was found under the hood. A black-and-gold "Special Edition" Trans Am joined the lineup, inspired by the similarly decorated 1976 Trans Am that celebrated Pontiac's 50th anniversary. The look was incredibly popular, helped no doubt by this model's central role in the 1977 motion picture *Smokey and the Bandit*. Trans Am sales came to 68,745, including 15,567 of the black-and-gold beauties.

PONTIAC ANNOUNCES:
THE WORLD'S ONLY TURBOCHARGED V-8

Wouldn't you know Pontiac would offer the world's first turbo V-8 production cars of the '80s. That's right. Pontiac's 1980 Trans Am and Formula Firebird are the only two production cars now available with a turbocharged V-8 gas engine.

The result is breathtaking.

You'll appreciate the turbo advantage of extra power available when you need it. And the way this engine moves smoothly into turbo boost. (Firebirds are equipped with GM-built engines produced by various divisions. See your dealer for details.)

The cars themselves are as extraordinary as the engine. Both the new Trans Am and the sleekly sophisticated Formula Firebird cut corners with quick ratio power steering. Both can tame roads with a special available handling package that includes four-wheel disc brakes and rally suspension. And both cars are controlled from a cockpit that features bucket seats, console shifter and rally gage instrumentation.

Put the world's only production turbocharged V-8 cars through their paces at your nearby Pontiac dealer's soon.

MPG More Pontiac Excitement FOR THE Great Ones

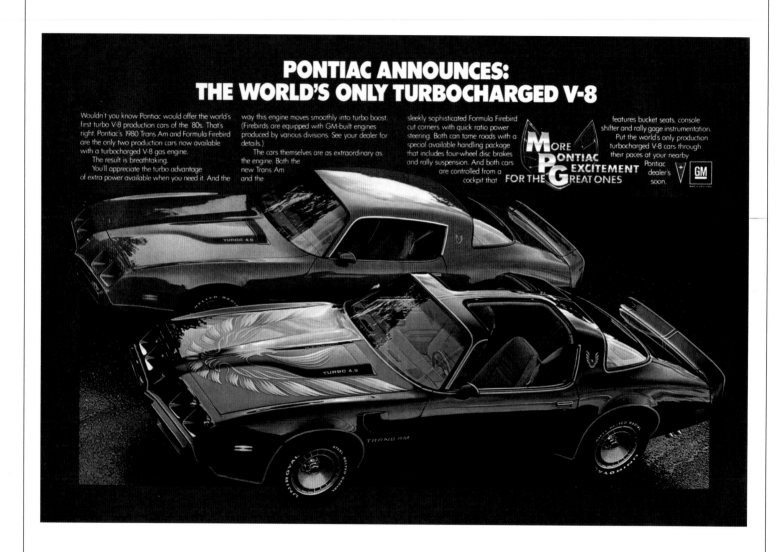

1980
TURBO TRANS AM

Firebird received another facelift in 1979. Engine offerings were cut dramatically in the look-alike 1980 models, with the 350-, 400-, and 403-inch offerings discontinued. The biggest mill was now a Chevy 305, rated at a lackluster 150 horsepower. Not satisfied, Pontiac decided to turbocharge its own 301-cube V-8. Offered in both Formula and Trans Am, the blown 301 was good for 210 ponies. A 1980 Turbo Trans Am was chosen to pace that year's Indy 500, and Pontiac promptly produced 5700 replicas. All were decked out with white and gray paint, white dished wheels, oyster interior, and specific race-day graphics. Trans Ams still had the traditional engine-turned instrument-panel surround, and turbocharged models had a special hood with an offset bulge and indicator lights.

1989

20TH ANNIVERSARY TRANS AM

Firebird was downsized for 1982, with the third-generation model shrinking to a 101-inch wheelbase and losing more than eight inches in length and 500 pounds in weight. For Trans Am's 20th anniversary in 1989, Pontiac released a special gift for the model's fans: an anniversary edition with a turbocharged 3.8-liter V-6 under the hood. Last seen in Buick's sizzling Grand National and GNX, the 250-horsepower turbo cranked out an imposing 340 lb/ft of torque. One of the most potent Trans Ams ever built, the 20th Anniversary model came only with automatic shift. No crass graphics marred the white body, adorned by nothing more than subtle "20th Anniversary" cloisonné emblems and "Turbo Trans Am" badges. A stock example served as the Pace Car for the 1989 Indy 500.